Designing Experiences

Designing Experiences

J. Robert Rossman and

Mathew D. Duerden

Foreword by B. Joseph Pine II

Columbia Business School
Publishing

Columbia University Press
Publishers Since 1893
New York Chichester, West Sussex
cup.columbia.edu

Library of Congress Cataloging-in-Publication Data
Names: Rossman, J. Robert (James Robert), 1946- author. |
Duerden, Mathew D., author.
Title: Designing experiences / J. Robert Rossman, Mathew D. Duerden.
Description: New York : Columbia University Press, [2019] |
Includes bibliographical references and index.
Identifiers: LCCN 2019004424 (print) | LCCN 2018061290 (e-book) |
ISBN 9780231191685 (cloth : alk. paper) | ISBN 9780231549516 (e-book)
Subjects: LCSH: Customer relations. | Customer services. | Experience. |
Target marketing.
Classification: LCC HF5415.5 .R675 2019 (e-book) |
LCC HF5415.5 (print) | DDC 658.5/038—dc23
LC record available at https://lccn.loc.gov/2019004424

Columbia University Press books are printed on permanent
and durable acid-free paper.
Printed in the United States of America

Cover design: Noah Arlow

Contents

Foreword

B. JOSEPH PINE II

I FIRST MET Mat Duerden in 2017 at the annual thinkAbout event that my partner Jim Gilmore and I had staged every year for the past twenty years. A couple of Brigham Young University colleagues had come the previous year, and one of them joined Mat at this, our final event in Cleveland. It was from Mat that we heard the news: thanks to their collective and concerted efforts, BYU had changed the name of their program from the "Department of Recreation Management" to the "Department of Experience Design and Management"! It is the first university in the United States I know of to fully recognize the importance of *experience* design and management.

And this book, by Mat and his colleague Bob Rossman, is the first I know of that is fully focused on putting forth a set of experience design ideas, principles, and frameworks that will, should you follow them, yield an intentionally designed and engagingly staged experience.

Now, truth be told, I am still looking forward to meeting the lead author, but based on what you will read here, I know Bob understands experience design. Interestingly, in the very first chapter where Bob and Mat discuss applying *user* experience design, *customer* experience design, and *service* experience design, I half-expected them to direct the reader to apply *experience* experience design, for that should be the focus: the design of the actual experience that people have. For as my partner Jim and I endeavored to make clear in our book *The Experience Economy*, experiences are a distinct economic offering, as distinct from services as services are from goods. Experiences use goods as props and services as the stage to engage each individual in

an inherently personal way and thereby create a memory, the hallmark of the experience.

In guiding experience designers to make that a reality Bob and Mat focus on three factors I consider paramount in the field: being intentional, orchestrating elements, and designing time.

The authors introduce the concept of intentionality right up front. People have many experiences throughout life that are unplanned, and companies offer many experiences that are haphazardly designed or even totally unplanned. But to have any success in today's experience economy, you must be very intentional about what it is you are staging, about what you want your guests—the customers of experiences—to undergo in order to engage them and create that memory.

Here the authors usefully apply the notions of micro- and macroexperiences, where the intentional design of the microexperiences—the deliberate sequencing of engaging elements—add up to the macroexperience encompassing the phases of anticipation (before), participation (during), and reflection (after). In *The Experience Economy* we discuss this intentionality at its highest level under the concept of an experience theme—the organizing principle of the experience that lets you, as the designer, determine what is in the experience and what is out in order to stage a cohesive experience, one that hangs together across all the microexperiences to form, define, and sequence that macroexperience. (And as an aside, you've got to love a book that introduces as the masters of intentionality the proprietors of Buc-ee's restroom experiences! But you have to be in Texas to truly appreciate them.)

You can see this focus on intentionality right in Mat and Bob's definition of experience design: "the process of *intentionally* orchestrating experience elements to provide opportunities for participants to co-create and sustain interactions that lead to results desired by the participant and the designer." And right there, too, you see the second key factor mentioned earlier: orchestrating. Although Jim Gilmore and I tend to use the term *stage*, we have always understood that *orchestrate* and even *choreograph* fit as well, for they each describe how that intentionality results itself in the design of every aspect of the experience, from the environment to the positive cues arrayed in that environment (as well as the negative cues absent, sometimes conspicuously so), to what workers do to enable each guest to fully

engage in each experience and create that memory—all of which Bob and Mat collectively and helpfully dub the *experiencescape.*

The third factor is the one I fully appreciated only years after our book was published in 1999—namely, that experience design is fundamentally the design of time. Each microexperience takes up its own particular amount of time; orchestrating the length and sequence of the microexperiences builds them up over time, drawing guests through a timeline that finally yields the macroexperience; and doing all this intentionally generates the drama you want to create—and be—in the world.

In fact, I love that in chapter 8 the authors discuss dramatic structure and introduce the Freytag diagram, something we, too, added to the updated edition of *The Experience Economy* in 2011. For the Freytag diagram—the brainchild of nineteenth-century German performance theorist Gustav Freytag—is something theater students learn to this day to understand and embrace drama. This framework leads you in designing time, to put together that sequence of events, one on top of the other, that rise in action, build up to the climax, and then come back down again as the experience draws to a close. Without drama, the sequence falls flat, without much of anything going on. Ah, but with drama, your intentionally designed experience fully engages each guest to leave the residue of memory within them. Drama is time well designed.

That right there, by the way, is why I've also grown to despise the term *customer experience.* For as used by most everybody, it means to make interactions with customers nice, easy, and convenient. True, distinctive experiences, however, must be memorable, personal, and revealed over a duration of time—in other words, must have drama.

Being convenient is the antithesis of an experience as a distinct economic offering, for it results in spending *less* time with customers, rather than getting customers to value the time they spend with you, and want to spend more of it. Nice, easy, and convenient are *service* characteristics, not experience characteristics. They are all well and good when what you want to do is deliver a service, one that provides customers with time well saved. But experiences are about offering time well spent, and to do that you must intentionally orchestrate microexperiences across the breadth of time guests spend with you—design the drama of time—to yield that macroexperience of an engaging experience.

To do that well, I urge you to follow the prescriptions of Bob and Mat here in *Designing Experiences.* You will reap the rewards in your experience offerings, in your business, and in your life.

B. Joseph Pine II
Dellwood, Minnesota
Co-founder, Strategic Horizons LLP

Author, *The Experience Economy*, *Authenticity*, *Mass Customization*, and *Infinite Possibility: Creating Customer Value on the Digital Frontier*

Preface

Thanks for Joining Us!

OVER THE LAST twenty years a lot has been written about the importance of experiences for individuals and organizations. Think about how and why experiences matter to you personally. You most likely attempt to fill your life with positive experiences. You also probably seek out companies that in addition to providing you with goods and services also deliver great experiences. While living in Texas, Mat would drive an extra few miles to shop at his favorite grocery store, H-E-B, even though there were other grocery stores closer to his home. He gladly did so because of the superior experience H-E-B delivered.

In an economy increasingly driven by the quality of experiences provided, organizations that deliver great experiences to customers and employees thrive and those that don't become obsolete. Good experiences attract and retain loyal customers and employees, whereas bad experiences either drive them away or fail to motivate repeat business. A widely adopted business truth can, in fact, be seen in the prevalent use of the word "experience" by a wide range of companies, from Adobe's tagline "Make experience your business" to Delta's promotion of "the Delta experience," everyone's talking about experience. What we found surprising is that although "experience" is getting a lot of air time, there's very little guidance available on how to systematically design experiences.

We believe there is a need for a book that clearly lays out a process to design experiences from beginning to end. It is not enough to bear witness to the profitability of experiences or their wonderful contributions to individuals and society, to work in this field you need to be

able to design them. The book you're holding, *Designing Experiences*, represents our effort to fill this gap.

Why We're Interested in Experiences

Your authors, Bob and Mat, have been engaged in designing and delivering leisure and educational experiences for more than forty years combined. We both have a PhD in leisure studies and have worked as face-to-face leaders, supervisors, and managers of organizations whose goal was to deliver leisure experiences. Leisure is the gold standard of experience design because leisure experiences are freely chosen and intrinsically motivated. When designing great leisure experiences, you quickly learn that you're involved in a joint venture with your participants. If the experiences you design don't fit with your participants' perceptions of what leisure means to them, they will quickly go elsewhere. We strongly believe that the lessons we've learned about leisure experiences and the tools we've developed to design them have relevance for all experience design contexts. We are excited to be a part of this emerging field and to see the work we have enjoyed for so many years more broadly applied.

Bob completed an undergraduate degree in recreation from Indiana University. At his first job in the Village of Oak Park, Illinois, he was responsible for operating special events. The event plans he inherited were mostly checklists of necessary supplies and scheduling information. There was nothing about what was supposed to happen to the individuals as a result of participating in these events. He started pondering what unique experiences he would expect if he were coming to one of these events and what it would take to ensure that these experiences occurred. He then challenged his staff to do the same. They liked thinking this way, and doing so became a standard operating procedure. They learned first to identify the experiences intended and then to design the encounters, interactions, and staging necessary to produce the experiences intended. Since his first position in Oak Park, Bob has focused his career on building and refining techniques to accomplish this basic proposition.

Mat started thinking about experience design while floating down the Main Salmon and Middle Fork of the Salmon Rivers in central Idaho. During high school and college Mat worked as a guide on

five-to-seven-day whitewater trips for his father's rafting company. Mat often noticed significant changes in participants' behaviors and relationships over the course of a trip. Stress dissipated, people laughed and talked with each other more, and individuals who started the trip as strangers quickly developed meaningful friendships. As Mat observed these and other positive changes, he started to wonder what it was about a multiday river trip that facilitated these changes. Was it the magnificent natural setting, the physically challenging nature of the activities, or the disconnect from society and technology? His pondering the nature of these experiences on the river eventually started him down a pathway of research, teaching, and practice focused on experiences and their design.

There is no generally accepted volume that defines fundamental concepts of experience design, anchors these concepts in social science literature, and provides pragmatic, usable tools for designing experiences. In writing this book, we've done our best to integrate some of our favorite experience design tools with insights and approaches gleaned from some of the top contemporary experience thinkers like Joe Pine, Jim Gilmore, Martin Seligman, Tom and David Kelly, Chip and Dan Heath, Mihaly Csikszentmihalyi, Daniel Kahneman, and Walt Disney. The techniques presented in this book are robust and will enable you to design new experiences as well as deconstruct, analyze, and redesign existing ones.

Understanding the social and psychological phenomena that facilitate experiences will help you better design them. Don't worry, we don't get too deep into theory, just enough to keep you on target to design experiences that people will find engaging. The majority of the book deals with specific techniques that we have used and taught to students for more than twenty-five years. We also integrate design thinking as an excellent approach for infusing innovation into the overall experience design process. We believe you will find these topics very practical in performing your day-to-day work of designing experiences.

We owe thanks to a lot of people who helped in various ways to bring this book to life. Foremost, we would like to thank our families and especially our wives, Linda Rossman and Chenae Duerden, respectively, for their support in our writing this book and throughout our careers. We had some excellent undergraduate students, including Sydney Burgess, Catherine Gardiner, and Madie Smith,

who provided feedback on early versions of the book. A number of our academic colleagues, including Dr. Gary Ellis at Texas A&M University, Dr. Barbara Schlatter at Illinois State University, and the faculty in the Department of Experience Design and Management at Brigham Young University, have influenced our thinking about experiences and have also provided valuable feedback during the writing of this book. We are sure they will find included in the book some of the ideas they have shared during discussions with us. The book is better for their generous input.

We want to thank B. Joseph Pine II for both his pioneering efforts to bring attention to the experience economy and for graciously agreeing to write a foreword for this book. We are also grateful to Myles Thompson, editor at Columbia Business School Publishing, who believed in us and our book project from the beginning. He and Brian Smith have been supportive and most helpful in improving and completing this book. Finally, we want to thank you for taking the time to read our book, and we wish you good luck in your own experience design endeavors.

J. Robert Rossman (Bob)
Phoenix, AZ
Mathew D. Duerden (Mat)
Provo, UT

Designing Experiences

PART ONE

Understanding Experience

EVERYONE WANTS TO BE part of the experience economy these days. The word *experience* is added as an adjective to almost everything (e.g., dining experiences, check-in experiences, employee on boarding experiences). Simply adding the word *experience*, though, does not automatically make something a worthwhile experience. In this section we examine the concepts of experience and experience design and develop definitions that are grounded but pragmatic; these are definitions experience designers can use to guide their work. Our examination of the psychology of experience will help you understand the behavioral nature of experience and what makes a great one. Finally, we provide a framework of experience types from prosaic to transformational that will prepare you for comprehensive experience design. This section will deepen your understanding of experiences and give you the background you will need to develop immersive and engaging experiences.

CHAPTER ONE

Exploring Experiences and Experience Design

WHAT DO THE following companies have in common?

- USAA
- Costco
- Ritz Carlton
- JetBlue
- H-E-B
- Amazon
- Apple
- Netflix

This is a diverse group of organizations. Some offer products and others provide services. The reason they're on this list is because they each hold the title of Net Promoter Score® (NPS) leader for 2018 in their various industries.[1] NPS is a measurement tool developed by Bain & Company's Fred Reichheld to assess customer brand loyalty.[2] The score is calculated by having customers respond on a 0–10 scale to this question: "How likely would you be to recommend [company]

to a friend or colleague?" If customers answer with a 9 or 10, they're promoters; if their answer is between 0 and 6, they're detractors. You then subtract the percentage of total detractors from total promoters to calculate your score. In general, although benchmarks vary across industries, an excellent NPS is above 50.[3]

Here's the previous list of companies along with their NPS scores:

- USAA: 79
- Costco: 79
- Ritz Carlton: 75
- JetBlue: 74
- H-E-B: 72
- Amazon: 68
- Apple: 63
- Netflix: 62

These organizations consistently convert customers into loyal brand ambassadors. How do they do it? We believe the primary driver behind their NPS success is the experience they deliver to customers. Whether it's selling entertainment in the case of Netflix or consumer goods in the case of Costco, these companies have figured out how to design and consistently deliver powerfully positive customer experiences. Experiences matter across all industries. Companies that provide great experiences to customers and employees succeed; those that don't, fail. Experiences matter in our personal lives as well. They shape our identities and affect relationships with friends and families. This book aims to help you understand the inner workings of experiences and how to design them. Great experiences don't happen serendipitously—they require intentionality and planning. In this book we're going to introduce you to the insights and tools you need to become an excellent experience designer.

You are an experience designer whether or not you realize it. You are constantly involved in authoring experiences for your customers, colleagues, friends, and family. The relevant question is, Are you doing this intentionally? Conscious and purposeful experience design is a key to personal and professional success. Although some people (e.g., Walt Disney) and organizations (e.g., Ritz Carlton) appear to have the innate ability to deliver amazing experiences, the experiences they deliver are in fact built on a foundation of meticulous and

intentional design. While we can't guarantee that reading this book will turn you into the next Walt Disney, we strongly believe that anyone can become a competent experience designer.

Experiences Matter

If you are reading this book, you're probably already on board with the idea that experiences matter. Even so, we want to review some of the primary reasons we think everyone should pay more attention to experiences. Experiences power our modern economy. B. Joseph Pine II and James H. Gilmore have been spreading the message of the experience economy since the mid-1990s.[4] Over the last 150 years we have moved from an agrarian economy driven by harvesting commodities like corn and coal, to an industrial economy built on manufacturing goods, to a service economy consisting of delivering services, to our current experience economy, where the central economic activity is designing experiences. It's an economy where consumers make purchasing decisions based not simply on product features but also on the experiences they facilitate.

The companies listed earlier in the chapter convert customers into promoters in large part because of the quality of the experiences they provide. Pine and Gilmore's classic example of this economic progression is the escalating price point moving from unprocessed coffee beans (commodity), to coffee grounds (product), to a generic cup of coffee (service), and finally to a high-end cup of Starbucks coffee (experience).[5] In essence, people are willing to pay more for the same basic product if it's wrapped in a desirable experience.

This economic progression involves transitioning economic activity from delivering a service to providing an engaging experience. A continuing controversy is whether experience is different from service or simply a different kind of service. We think it is different. A service is a unique category of economic activity. In some cases, the service being purchased is access to a special piece of equipment or skill in using it—for example, sharpening ice skates. One can obtain a hand sharpener and do it oneself, but a good sharpening requires a special machine and skill in using it. Other services involve hiring someone to do an unpleasant task like washing windows. This can be performed by the homeowner because it does not require special skill. But people employ

others to do the service because they do not have time or do not like to do the job.

An experience differs in that it requires the customer to be consciously engaged and the engagement is sustained through volitional actions of the participant. Consider the monikers used to describe the recipients of each. Service organizations think of their customers as guests, clients, patients, etc., all implying that something needs to be done for them. Experience-producing organizations think of their customers as participants. The technology writer Clay Shirky points out, "Participants are different. To participate is to act as if your presence matters, as if, when you see something or hear something, your response is part of the event."[6] Experience demands conscious attention, engagement, and action—in a word, participation. The experiences we are preparing you to design will be immersive and engaging, requiring attention and action by the participant.

Supersizing service does not transform it to an experience. For example, hotels now speak of not just serving but pampering their visitors. Such an approach still remains a service; the provider is doing something to or for the client, now even more intently. Although a supersized service may be intense, its effects are usually fleeting and must be purchased again. Service is sustained by the provider instead of the participant; even so, service provision needs to be high quality. We discuss attributes of high-quality services, which we define as technical factors (see chapter 9). Almost all the experiences discussed in this book contain service components that need to be delivered well to enhance the experience, but they are not the experience.

Let's now consider the importance of engaging experiences on a more personal level. Consider the following thought exercise shared with us by our good friend and colleague Dr. Gary Ellis, who is a leading experience design scholar at Texas A & M University.[7]

1. Think of some of your most cherished memories. Invariably, many of these have to do with specific experiences you've had.
2. Now decide a price it would take for you to be willing to part with these memories.

What number did you come up with—$50, $500, $5,000, or $50,000? Have you set a higher price? In many cases when individuals are asked

this question, they refuse to name an amount because they could never imagine parting with important memories. We value our most precious memories, and these memories come from our experiences. Research conducted by Paul Ratner and by Elizabeth Dunn and Michael Norton shows that spending money on experiences has a greater, long-lasting effect on happiness levels than spending money on material goods.[8] We may experience a momentary rush, like a sugar high, from purchasing a product, but the novelty and the importance of that item will invariably fade with time. In contrast, investing in experiences leads to increased returns because memories of positive experiences ripen and become even more important when recalled and reflected on over time.

As important as it is to design and deliver good experiences, it's perhaps even more important, especially in our digitally connected world, to avoid negative customer experiences. In other words, you want to avoid an experience becoming memorable because it was a bad one! In the pre-social-media world, when companies delivered bad experiences, the only people who heard about them were usually the close friends and associates of the recipient of the experience. Now, bad experiences are broadcast to the world through social media.[9]

Consider the case of Dave Carroll, whose guitar was damaged on a United Airlines flight. After the airline refused to pay for the damages, he and his band made a music video about the experience that garnered over sixteen million views on YouTube. The fallout from this one experience purportedly cost United Airlines millions.[10] As you read this, you're probably thinking of examples of the latest negative customer or employee experience to go viral. Companies can no longer hope the occasional poorly delivered customer experience will simply go away; good experiences need to be consistently delivered to build and maintain customer loyalty, and bad ones need to be quickly repaired.

Companies are also beginning to realize that the experiences they provide for their employees are as important as those they provide for their customers. In their *2017 Global Human Capital Trends* report for Deloitte Insights, Josh Bersin and his colleagues note that improving the employee experience was identified as the fourth most important trend in rewriting employment rules for the digital age: "Today, companies are looking at employee journeys, studying the needs of their workforce, and using net promoter scores to understand the employee experience."[11] They also assert that good employee

experiences translate into good customer experiences. Paychecks and standard benefits are no longer enough to attract top applicants in competitive industries. Just like prospective customers, employees are also looking for great experiences.

The bottom line is that experiences matter. On an organizational level, well-designed experiences can help companies build customer loyalty, attract and retain employees, and rise above the competition. They are so important that experience and experience outcomes are now included as strategic outcomes for corporations. Although this book is focused on developing the ability to design and deliver experiences at the individual interactional level, we do provide some examples of their inclusion in corporate strategic planning (see chapter 10). On a personal level, great experiences are what make life enjoyable and meaningful. While some great experiences happen spontaneously, the consistent delivery of high-quality experiences requires knowledgeable, intentional experience design. Creating great experiences is also personally rewarding work; it is an endeavor we think you'll enjoy as much as we do.

What Are Experiences?

Because so many people are talking about experiences right now, you would think everyone is on the same page regarding what experiences actually are. To illustrate this point, ask a few people the question, "What is an experience?" More than likely, you will get a different answer from each person. Although experiences are commonplace, they are also complex, making defining them a bit tricky. Often, people will provide an example of an experience they have had rather than defining the actual phenomenon of experiences. Examples are not definitional. The lack of an accepted definition is a bit concerning to us because it's hard to design something that you cannot define.

In some cases, attempts to define experiences focus on describing the context (e.g., customer, leisure, educational) in which the experience occurs. While it is true that these context-based experiences have certain unique characteristics, such a categorization falls short of providing a generalizable definition of experience. The English language also makes defining experiences difficult. Whereas other languages,

like German, have multiple terms for *experience*, English assigns multiple meanings to the same word.[12] For example, *experience* can mean "knowledge or skill acquired from cumulative exposure" (as in "I have twenty years' experience in my field") or "past events that represent a shared community" (as in "the American experience").

For our purposes, we're interested in *experience* in the sense of something you personally accomplish, something that you do to affect outcomes, or something that makes you feel a certain way (e.g., "I had a great experience playing tennis"). This more active form implies conscious awareness of and engagement with what's happening around you. Interestingly, the word *experience* originates from the Latin *experiri*, which means "to try or to attempt"; it denotes active engagement.[13]

Defining Experience

Now that we've discussed some basic features of experiences, we will turn our attention to developing a working definition of experience. In its simplest form, experience is consciousness of ongoing interaction. The experiences we discuss in this book require reciprocal interaction between individuals and their surroundings. This interaction must be sustained by the deliberate engagement of the individuals participating in the experience. They are immersive, engaged experiences, not passive ones resulting from service encounters. For an experience to occur, you have to be aware that something is happening around you and you're contributing to the resulting outcomes. Our primary interest is in more complex experiences, the kind of experiences that turn customers into ambassadors and employees into advocates. To build an actionable definition of experience, we need to briefly discuss a few additional components of experiences (see figure 1.1).[14]

First, experiences are multiphased: each experience consists of an anticipation phase, a participation phase, and a reflection phase. Second, within each phase, multiple sequential interactions occur between the participant and the elements of the designed experience. We'll provide a more detailed discussion of these elements in chapter 4 because these are the primary building blocks you will need to take account of or manipulate when designing experiences. For now, you should think of these elements as the people, places, and things that

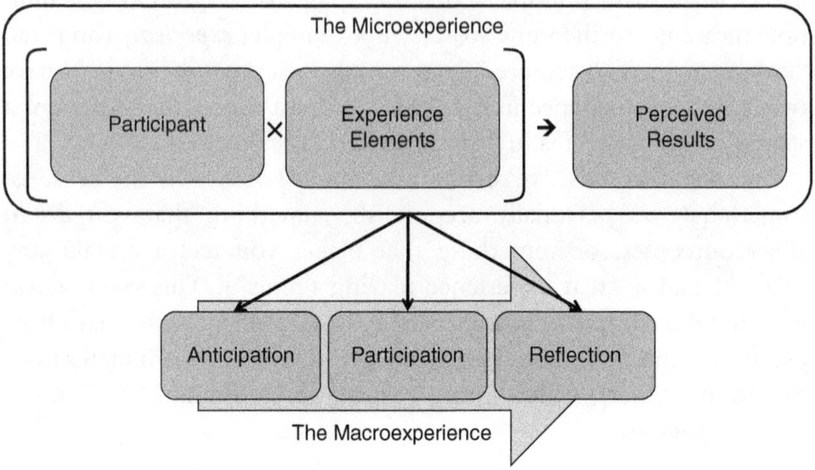

Figure 1.1 Foundational experience components. Modified from Mat D. Duerden, Peter J. Ward, and Patti A. Freeman, "Experiences: Seeking Interdisciplinary Integration," *Journal of Leisure Research* 47, no. 5 (2015), 612.

make up the experience. Third, interactions between the participant and the elements of the experience co-create a variety of potential results driven largely by the participant's perceptions and reactions in the experience. These perceptions, labeled "perceived results" in figure 1.1, could include thoughts, emotions, attitudes, or behaviors. They are minded outcomes resulting from intentional reflection triggered by active engaged participation in the experience.

Combining the foundational components in figure 1.1, we offer the following definition of experience: *Experience is a unique interactional phenomenon resulting from conscious awareness and reflective interpretation of experience elements that is sustained by a participant, culminating in personally perceived results and memories.*

Experiences present in two formats: micro- and macroexperiences. Microexperiences are discrete interactional episodes across the *anticipation*, *participation*, and *reflection phases* that together constitute the cumulative macroexperience. The macro/microexperience designation is based on the elevation from which you view the experience. A single vacation could be seen as a microexperience if the perspective is the full life experience of an individual, or it could be broken down into all the microexperiences that occurred during the vacation.

It's important to understand that you often will find yourself switching between these two perspectives as you design experiences. We'll have more to say about this in chapters 5 and 6.

Using Foundational Experience Components: An Example

Consider how we can use the experience components just introduced to deconstruct a fairly commonplace experience like going to a restaurant. During the *anticipation phase* of this experience, you begin thinking about going out for dinner. You probably start by considering what type of food you would like, whom you would like to go with, the price you would like to pay, and where you might like to go. If you're always looking for the next great place to eat, you may look at restaurant reviews and menus online. All these thought processes and decisions represent interactions between you and the elements of the experience, including those provided by external entities (e.g., restaurant review apps, social media posts, online menus) and those of your own making (e.g., friends you want to invite, your mode of transportation to the restaurant, your budget). One of these will likely be the principal driver of your decision making. For example, you primarily want to go to dinner with friends, and where you go and what is served are of less importance.

The transition from the *anticipation phase* to the *participation phase* usually occurs as you begin to interact with elements of the actual experience. In our example, this could include microexperiences like arriving at and walking into the restaurant. It deserves noting that the subjective results of the anticipation phase spill over into the participation phase. For example, if you read some great reviews about the restaurant, you will likely bring a positive attitude as you enter the participation phase. If you called ahead and made a reservation, the host will greet you with a reserved table for you and your friends. The interaction between your positive attitude about the restaurant and the expedited seating process will most likely produce continued positive feelings about the experience—or in the language of our experience definition, a *positive perceived result.* It's also easy to imagine how the perceived outcome of this initial participation phase could be different if you had read negative reviews about the restaurant, the restaurant didn't take reservations, or you were not given a suitable welcome by the host. Additional microexperiences

like ordering, receiving, and eating food; talking with friends; and paying for your meal also occur during the participation phase. For an account of how some restaurant corporations think about and design the interactions in a dining experience, see the Fox Restaurant Concepts and Brinker International entries in chapter 10.

After leaving the restaurant, you enter the *reflection phase* of the experience, and your perceived results from the participation phase will influence your perceived outcome of the overall experience. This transition is marked by a switch from engaging in the actual experience to reflecting on what happened. The reflection phase is especially relevant after you experience something very negative or very positive. Most of your life experiences have short, weak reflection phases because they aren't especially memorable. But for those that are either very good or very bad, the reflection phase often includes conversations about the experience with others, either in person or through social media; looking at pictures taken during the experience; or simply reflecting back on the experience. One's summary judgment about the experience is malleable at this point and influenced by the internalized narrative of personal reflection as well as discussions with others who participated. The perceived results of the reflection phase often determine whether you consider returning to the restaurant again, which brings you back to the anticipation phase, where the process begins anew. The experience loop terminates if you decide to never return.

As you can see, experiences—even those as familiar as going out to eat—are complex, and designing them is an intricate and involved process. It requires more than simply giving lip service to the importance of customer service. Designing experiences requires an intentional, tested process to create experiences that will lead participants through a sequence of interactions across all three experience phases, interactions that produce results desired by the participant and intended by the experience designer. The tools and knowledge we include in later chapters will provide a methodology for designing experiences to produce the results desired.

What Is Experience Design?

Now that we've defined *experience*, let's turn our attention to defining *experience design*. Increased interest in experiences has led to multiple

experience design approaches. You may have heard such terms as *user experience design*, *customer experience design*, and *service experience design*, to name a few. Each of these refers to the application of the experience design process within a specific context:

- User experience design (UX design) focuses on the design of human-computer interactions.
- Customer experience design deals with the design of customer-company interactions.
- Service experience design involves intentionally creating effective and positive service encounters.

Specialization within experience design is important because the nuances of each context warrant some degree of customization. For example, in UX design there is a continuing issue about the locus of the experience. Is the experience the interaction with the computer, or is the computer simply a window that provides a conduit to the experience? Unique contextual issues aside, there are more commonalities than differences across these fields, but limited communication between them and the lack of a shared foundation are problematic.

The experience design writer Brian Solis had the following to say about this disconnect: "It's rare for specialists in these several disciplines [brand experience, customer experience, and user experience] to interact, and even less common for companies to integrate them in experience design efforts. This is a travesty, as they have much to share with each other."[15] For the most part, these subdisciplines of experience design have developed independently of one another and without efforts to identify common ground on which all could build.

Innovation often works this way, with new ideas emerging independently and simultaneously. The sociologist Robert Merton called this phenomenon "multiple discoveries." Long lists of these simultaneous innovations exist, such as calculus, the theory of evolution, and the atomic bomb. Multiple discoveries seem to occur "when prerequisite kinds of knowledge and tools accumulate in man's cultural store, and when the attention of an appreciable number of investigators becomes focused on a problem."[16]

The simultaneous development of experience design subfields came about as individuals and industries became aware of the importance of experiences and realized that they needed to take steps to approach

their design more intentionally. An example of this is the recent trend of organizations' creating the position of chief experience officer because they know delivering great experiences is important yet they do not fully know what they want individuals in this position to do.[17] Although an increasing recognition of the need for an experience design methodology exists, consensus is still lacking on what exactly experience design is or should be. As Peter Benz noted in his book *Experience Design: Concepts and Case Studies*, "The full potential of experience design as a distinct creative discipline in its own right still needs to be articulated and recognized."[18] Experience design should be defined in a generalizable way that positions it as the foundational field of all its related subfields (e.g., user experience, customer experience, service experience). This book makes an effort to define experience design and present its key tenets and tools in a way that promotes broad applicability.

Before revealing our proposed definition of experience design, let's look at the meaning of the words *experience* and *design*. The previous section dealt with the term *experience* at length, but as a reminder, some key elements to its definition include its multiphased nature, conscious awareness, and the interaction between participants and experience elements leading to perceived results. *Design* is a word like *experience*, with multiple meanings depending on its usage. We like the definition provided by Harold G. Nelson and Erik Stolterman in their insightful book *The Design Way*. They view design as "the ability to imagine that-which-does-not-yet-exist, to make it appear in concrete form as a new, purposeful addition to the real world."[19] When you engage in design, you intentionally create something in order to produce a desired change, a planned intervention with a purposeful intention.

By combining the concepts we've shared for experience and design, we offer the following definition of experience design: *Experience design is the process of intentionally orchestrating experience elements to provide opportunities for participants to co-create and sustain interactions that lead to results desired by the participant and the designer.* Experiences are complex and ever present, but to create experiences that truly stand out and produce intended results, someone must intervene in a purposeful way. That someone should be an experience designer, and that designer could be you.

Summary: Let's Get Going

We've set the stage with definitions for experience and experience design. We hope that you now recognize the complexities of experiences and the interactive process whereby experiences produce results. Anyone can schedule a get-together for a group of people, and in the process of interacting, some outcome will result. But the act of designing and delivering an experience that produces results valued by the participant and the provider requires an intentional process. Our goal in the chapters that remain is to give you the knowledge and tools you need to design experiences in any context and for any population. This is an interdisciplinary field, and we draw from a variety of disciplines as we guide you along the path toward experience design expertise. We will also continually highlight the differences between experiences and services.

Before wrapping up this chapter, we want to make a couple of quick terminology-housekeeping comments. We will at times use the term *experience staging* or *experience stager* to refer, respectively, to the act of delivering an experience and to those individuals who facilitate the experience-staging process. Most of the time we use the term *experience stager* when we're referring to frontline employees who directly interact with end users. We will also use a few different terms to refer to the individuals who engage in the experiences you design, including *customer*, *participant*, and *end user*. We decided to use these terms interchangeably to reflect the diverse nature of the individuals for whom readers of this book will be designing experiences. Personally, we prefer *participant* because the word connotes the deliberate interaction needed for co-creation.

When you're done reading this book, you will be off to a good start on becoming an experience designer. You will have a grasp of foundational topics and tools that will allow you to design innovative, intentional experiences. Let's now move on to the next step on our experience design journey: a review of the work of some of the top sociopsychological thinkers about the phenomenon of experiences.

CHAPTER TWO

What Makes a Great Experience?

FOR A FEW summers while Mat was earning his master's degree, he and his wife, Chenae, codirected a wilderness adventure camp for disadvantaged adolescents in the mountains of central Idaho. One of the youth participants, whom we'll call Tom, was short and wiry with a massive mop of messy blonde hair. He showed up at camp with a skateboard, even though there was no place to skate, and a lot of energy. It was not easy to capture Tom's attention, and he was exasperating his counselors. One day as Mat was making his rounds through camp, one of the counselors came up to him and told him there was something he had to see.

It turned out to be Tom, who was standing perfectly still with his hand outstretched toward a hummingbird feeder hanging from a tree. The counselor told Mat that Tom's group had been learning about birds that day and had been told that if they put sugar water on their hand and held it very still by the feeder, a hummingbird might land on their hand. For whatever reason, this prospect had fascinated Tom so much that he was willing to stand still—something that had not yet happened during his waking hours at camp—for the chance of having

a hummingbird land on his hand. To his delight, it happened after a few minutes of waiting.

During this experience, Tom was fully in the moment. His attention was totally concentrated on the task at hand with little to no awareness of the world around him. Something about the chance to physically connect with a bird—with which he shared some similar behavioral patterns—captured and held his attention. Successful experience designers strive to deliver attention-captivating experiences like Tom's hummingbird encounter. The question is, How do you do this consistently? In this chapter we're going to look at a body of sociopsychological research to learn principles you can use to guide your experience design efforts.

What you will read in the remainder of this chapter may seem a bit obtuse to designing experiences. Trust us that this knowledge will help you design better and more intentional experiences. Too many in the field do not take the time to study the social psychology of experiencing before they begin designing experiences. This chapter will provide you with a deeper understanding of experiences and thereby make you a better designer of them.

Play and Flow

Our brains crave stimulation. It's why smartphones are so addicting—they're highly effective providers of visual and auditory stimulation as well interactive tactile and cognitive stimulation.[1] Our brains want us to interact with our environment so that we can learn, grow, and adapt. It's why kids need to play. In the late 1960s and early 1970s, Dr. Michael Ellis conducted observational studies of children in his Play Research Lab at the University of Illinois.[2] He was interested in understanding the motivations behind and outcomes resulting from unstructured play. Ellis's research showed that play provided children with a vehicle to obtain and maintain optimal levels of physical stimulation and cognitive arousal. Subsequent research has strengthened the case for play serving an essential developmental role for children and adults.[3]

Kids use play to find the sweet spot between understimulation (I'm bored) and overstimulation (I'm anxious). As adults, we also seek experiences that provide just the right amount of stimulation. You would

think that in a world with unending sources of stimulation, it would be easy to know how to pay attention to the types of experiences that would provide our brains with the right amount of feedback. Unfortunately, having too many choices actually impairs our decision-making ability and so we end up watching Netflix or engaging in other activities that tend to sedate rather than stimulate our brains.[4]

We all have had experiences, like Tom's hummingbird encounter, that have fully captured and held our attention. What is it about such experiences that make them so captivating? This question was, in part, what Mihaly Csikszentmihalyi set out to answer when he began studying the experiences of highly creative individuals.[5] Using a method called "experience sampling," which involved paging participants at random times during the day and having them complete a few questions about what they were doing and how they were feeling, Csikszentmihalyi discovered a common set of characteristics that study participants used to describe uniquely captivating experiences. He adopted the term *flow*, a word used frequently by respondents to label these types of experiences.

As Csikszentmihalyi's study of flow continued, he developed a list of descriptive characteristics of flow experiences. He also found that flow could occur in almost any context (work or leisure) and during any activity (from rock climbing to quilting) if the experience exhibited the following qualities:

- Clear goals—you know what you're trying to accomplish in the activity.
- Immediate feedback—you know how well you're doing in relation to the stated goals as you engage in the experience.
- Balance between challenge and skill—the experience provides the right amount of challenge in relation to your level of requisite skills.
- Merging of action and awareness—you are completely focused and engaged with the experience at hand.
- Loss of self-consciousness—you are so engrossed in the experience that you lose awareness of other things happening around you, including concern for what others may be thinking of you.
- Time becomes distorted—you lose complete track of time, and experiences that seem to take only minutes may actually have taken hours.
- Your participation is intrinsically motivated—you want to participate for the sake of the experience as opposed to some external reward.[6]

Think about Tom's experience with the hummingbird. Each of these qualities is clearly exhibited in that experience. He had a clear goal in mind, he received feedback in the form of the hummingbird's proximity to his hand throughout the experience, he was entirely focused on the experience, the activity provided him with a good balance between his skill level and the required challenge, he completely forgot about the world around him, he lost track of time, and he was intrinsically motivated.

The individuals for whom you are designing experiences are looking for experiences that capture their attention. We all want to find flow-producing experiences to fill at least portions of our day. As experience designers, we can use the insights about human experiences gleaned by researchers like Mike Ellis and Mihaly Csikszentmihalyi. Their work highlights that quality experiences occur only when individuals recognize and respond to what's happening around them. You have to catch people's attention and engage them if you want to provide them with a sustainable experience. Second, you need to find the sweet spot when designing and staging experiences in which you provide enough stimulation to catch and hold people's attention but not so much that they become overwhelmed, anxious, or confused. This means that you have to understand the people for whom you are providing experiences. What types of knowledge, skill levels, attitudes, and so on do they personally bring to the experience? You also need to understand some general principles of human psychology in order to design engaging, positive experiences.

What Do People Really Want to Experience?

Although experiences can produce a great variety of results, your first step in designing them is intentionally focusing on a finite number of specific desirable results that you have some probability of delivering. A classic mistake of experience design is to begin with *your* end in mind rather than what your participants want. Some organizations will have outcomes they want produced by the experiences they sponsor. For example, the YMCA (the Y) has specific organizational outcomes it desires from the programs it offers; the Y's three foci are youth development, healthy living, and social responsibility.[7] All the programs the Y offers are targeted to achieve one of these outcomes.

But participants' needs always deserve consideration because meeting participants' wants and solving their problems will have a strong influence on how they evaluate the experience and what they tell others about it. While acknowledging that every individual has unique needs, positive psychology offers insights into what results generally have the greatest positive effect and accordingly are most desired by participants.

In *Authentic Happiness*, Martin E. P. Seligman, the father of positive psychology, discusses the power of positive experiences. He states that "experiences that induce positive emotion cause negative emotion to dissipate rapidly."[8] This simple and straightforward statement is backed up by significant amounts of supportive research. Seligman also contends that happiness or positive emotion is only one component of healthy psychological functioning. Paul Dolan, in his book *Happiness by Design*, adds to this discussion by noting the need for purpose in addition to pleasure in the experiences we pursue. He introduces the pleasure-pain principle (PPP), which states that pleasure is contrasted with pain, and purpose is contrasted with pointlessness.[9] A life dilemma he discusses is the need to balance pleasure with purpose. Engaging only in pleasures without purpose does not make us feel good, nor does engaging only in purposeful activities.

Whom we engage with in experiences also matters. Seligman suggests that social bonding is a key facilitator of positive psychological functioning. In a study in which he and a colleague analyzed the very happiest 10 percent of college students from a pool of 222 students, social bonding was found to be a key differentiating factor. These "very happy" people differed markedly from individuals with average and low levels of happiness in one principal way: they enjoyed a rich and fulfilling social life. They spent the least amount of time alone (and the most time socializing), and they were rated highest on good relationships by themselves and their friends.[10] Dolan seconds this conclusion. After reviewing two large sets of happiness data from the United States and Germany, he concludes, "We can also show that we are again happier when we are interacting with other people."[11]

Chip and Dan Heath, in their book *The Power of Moments*, suggest shared experiences, especially those that allow people to struggle together while working to obtain a meaningful goal, build powerful and deep connections between individuals.[12] Think about those individuals in your own life you feel most connected to—we bet you've had the type of experiences with them that the Heath brothers are describing.

In Seligman's most recent book, *Flourish*, he introduced the PERMA model as a framework to present the necessary elements of optimal psychological functioning. He suggests that individuals live more fulfilling lives when they have experiences that produce the following results:[13]

- **Positive emotion**—leads to happiness. We all want to have experiences that produce positive emotions: the excitement of a first date, the joy of seeing a child take her first step, the satisfaction and savoring that comes from eating an expertly prepared meal.
- **Engagement**—a subjective state that draws heavily on flow theory and is present when individuals can answer affirmatively to such questions as " 'Did time stop for you?' 'Were you completely absorbed in the task?' 'Did you lose self-consciousness?' "[14] We all want and seek experiences that draw us in and engage our full attention.
- **Relationships**—we all need meaningful positive relationships with people who are important to us. Seligman states, "Very little that is positive is solitary. . . . Other people are the best antidotes to the downs of life and the single most reliable up."[15]
- **Meaning**—defined by Seligman as "belonging to and serving something that you believe is bigger than the self."[16] Meaning can be found in a career you consider to be a calling,[17] involvement in volunteer causes, or religiously motivated service, to name a few examples.
- **Accomplishment**—the pursuit of achievement for its own sake. This can be fulfilled in both the personal and the professional sphere. It represents a desire to develop domain mastery, not for praise or remuneration, but simply to gain a sense of competence.

The foregoing list is an important source of outcomes individuals are likely to desire in the experiences you design. They are abstract but universally applicable outcomes. Your job is to design experiences that allow participants to feel positive emotion, become engaged, build relationships, find meaning, and develop competence. If you can facilitate even one of these outcome categories with your experience, you're on the right track.

Research by Richard Ryan and Edward Deci[18] dovetails nicely with Seligman's work. Ryan and Deci propose that since we have

basic physical needs (e.g., food, shelter, water), we must also have basic psychological needs. Numerous studies support the conclusion, first proposed by Ryan and Deci, that to experience healthy psychological functioning, individuals need to experience adequate levels of autonomy, competence, and relatedness.[19] Autonomy is the sense that you have control over your actions and choices, competence is having the necessary skills for a particular activity, and relatedness is feeling connected with people who value and care about you. Ryan and Deci's research has shown that when basic psychological needs are met, people experience a variety of positive outcomes and feel a greater sense of intrinsic motivation.

The Psychology of Great Experiences

If we look at the findings from the research reviewed thus far in this chapter, we can draw a few relevant conclusions for experience designers. First, experiences are potential sources for the stimulation our brains need to promote development and healthy psychological functioning. Second, the best experiences accomplish the following:

- Produce positive emotions
- Engage attention
- Help develop and strengthen relationships
- Provide meaning through connections to something larger than ourselves
- Promote competence
- Grant autonomy

Although some experiences may facilitate everything on this list, such experiences are rare, and that's okay. We would become emotionally drained if every experience we had during the course of the day were meeting all those needs. This list provides experience designers a cafeteria of psychological outcomes they can draw from and incorporate into the experiences they are designing or already providing. For example, how can you tweak current experiences to provide more autonomy or design new experiences to better promote competence? There are countless results that may be targeted when designing experiences or improving the delivery of current ones. But the experiences

you design will be more meaningful if they encompass and facilitate at least some of the results discussed in this chapter.

Allocating Attention

So, you've gained some insights about what people need and want out of experiences. Don't forget that experiences exist only when they capture and sustain someone's conscious attention. You also know that the quality of the attention we give to things is not always the same. Consider the attention you would give on a hike to the song of a bird versus the rattling of a rattlesnake. One stimulus, the rattling, would most likely produce a higher degree of focused attention than the other stimulus, the song of a bird. The intensity of mental involvement in experiences was examined by Daniel Kahneman, who documented that the speed and intensity of thinking varies in different situations. He identifies two types of thinking:

- System 1 operates automatically and quickly, with little or no effort and no sense of voluntary control.
- System 2 allocates attention to the effortful mental activities that demand it, including complex computations. The operations of system 2 are often associated with the subjective experience of agency, choice, and concentration.[20]

System 1 thinking occurs quickly and involves little conscious attention. It makes up many of our daily experiences. In these experiences, information is familiar, routine, and quickly dealt with. These experiences do include cognitive awareness but not the rational processing of information that characterizes system 2 thinking. In our hiking example, hearing the song of a bird, a commonplace occurrence, would trigger system 1 thinking. We would most likely register hearing the song but wouldn't direct too much more attention to it than that.

Allow us a quick digression to illustrate how uniquely personal interpretations of stimuli can be. The previous scenario would not likely be true for individuals interested in ornithology. They would pay much more attention to the bird's song than other people and would likely spend some time identifying the bird's species. We digress to drive home the notion that estimating how individuals will react to the stimuli

provided in experiences can be difficult to predict accurately, and the more you know about participants, the better predictions you can make.

System 2 thinking is slower and more deliberate than system 1 thinking. It involves rational thought processing—the kind of interactive engagement likely needed to sustain interest and result in lasting memories. System 2 thinking is triggered by experiences that demand more concentrated attention like deciding which job offer to accept or how to respond to the nearby presence of a rattlesnake. Kahneman points out that many of our system 1 thoughts were derived at some point from system 2 deliberations. So, for him, system 2 is the key system because it provides a mechanism for memory. Each of us acquired our system 1 repertoire through our own history with system 2 experiences. Thus, you must remember when designing experiences that each person has a unique experiential history derived from previous system 2 interactions that he or she will use to process and perceive the experiences you provide.

Kahneman's work calls into question the notion that we should always be offering experiences that lead to lasting memories. This may be too large an order for routine daily production! Much of what we do each day—many of the touchpoints in an individual's journey—is likely to involve system 1 thinking, an unmemorable experience. This is confirmed by Chip and Dan Heath: "The surprise about great service experiences is that they are *mostly forgettable and occasionally remarkable*."[21] Yet, because of the admonishment of current literature, practitioners are badgered to offer memory-producing experiences that can result only from system 2 thinking. And not unexpectedly, given some of this new information, they are failing and frustrated.

Designing Memorable Experiences

The marketing and consumer-behavior literature is full of admonitions to deliver memorable experiences. Yet we find almost no discussion about the phenomenon of memory! Let's at least investigate it a little. A quick review of literature about memory informs us that memory is the process by which our brains encode, store, and retrieve information.[22] Without memory you would be lost, needing to relearn everything each day. We all generally understand the existence

of short-term versus long-term memory. Short-term is used during system 2 thinking, which requires us to remember multiple facts on a short-term basis to use during intense thinking and processing of information. The information that results from this processing is then selectively committed to our long-term memory for recall in the future as needed.

During experiences, you are consciously aware of many bits of incoming information being accessed through your five senses—taste, smell, sound, sight, and touch. You are aware of these information bits for a brief time and then select a few to use in your short-term memory for information processing. Through reflection and interpretation, you further select information to forget or to commit to long-term memory. Long-term memory is also known as declarative memory, which comprises facts and events that can be consciously recalled. There are two types of declarative memory: semantic, which is learned, and episodic, which is drawn from personal experience.

As Jennifer Ouellette notes, recent research has provided some interesting results about how experience in imprinted in our episodic memory:

> How the brain fixes the timing of the events we experience depends on episodic memory. Whenever you remember key events from your past, you are tapping into episodic memory, which encodes what happened, where it happened, and when it happened, doing so for all our remembered experiences. Neuroscientists know the brain must have a kind of internal clock or pacemaker to help it track those experiences and record them as memories.[23]

Researchers at the Kalvi Institute for Systems Neuroscience in Norway have discovered that experiences are not encoded or remembered in metric or circadian time as are most other events. How time in experiences is remembered differs fundamentally from how other kinds of temporal events are remembered.[24] Experiences are encoded in two separate areas of the brain, one area that records spatial information and the other that time stamps the order of events in an experience. These separate pieces of information are integrated in the hippocampus "to store a unified representation of what, where, and when."[25] This section of the brain's limbic system registers an experience by integrating the time order of what occurred and the space in which it occurred. In an article by Rita Elmkvist Nilsen, Kalvi Institute Researcher Albert

Tsao states, "The network (referring to the three areas of the brain that jointly accomplish this, *sic*) does not explicitly encode time. What we measure is rather a subjective time derived from the ongoing flow of experience."[26] It is interesting that Csikszentmihalyi also deduced this term *flow* from his work. Physiologically, experience is handled uniquely in our brain, not as other phenomena.

In the same article, Nilsen in reporting the work of the Kalvi research teams states, "Experience, and the succession of events within experience, are thus the substance of which subjective time is generated and measured by the brain."[27] Professor Edvar Moser, one of the researchers and a Nobel Prize recipient for his work in discovering how the brain accounts for space and our position within it, notes, "With this work, we have found an area with activity so strong relating to the time of an event or experience, it may open up a whole new research field."[28]

What does this mean for designing experiences? Your goal should be to create experiences that are memorable. Memorable experiences are recorded in episodic memory. Their physical location (the space they occupy) and the sequential separate engagements that constitute the experiences matter and become a part of a person's memory of them. The findings of this current research confirm that the techniques we are recommending matter in designing memorable experiences. Our speculation is that experiences likely to be memorable are those that occur in unique spaces and have special memorable engagements as part of their design that will facilitate future recall. Experience designers need to include both of these features in a design to ensure that experiences are memorable.

Producing Experiences?

It is well known that the interest in the concept of experience in business was initiated by the publication of B. Joseph Pine II and James H. Gilmore's *The Experience Economy: Work Is Theatre and Every Business a Stage*,[29] which was followed with an updated edition in 2011.[30] Pine and Gilmore introduced a major point of departure from existing thought—that experience is a fourth type of economic activity in addition to commodities, goods, and services and that experience is a unique differentiating factor consumers are willing

to pay for. Along these lines, the business writer Brian Solis suggests that "experiences are more important than products now. In fact, experiences are products."[31] In essence, if you're not providing great experiences, regardless of your industry, you will not survive.

Let's examine how Pine and Gilmore have raised awareness of the economic importance of experiences. Their concept of experience rests on three propositions. First, experiences are different from services. When a customer "buys an experience, he [or she] pays to spend time enjoying a series of memorable events that a company stages—as in a theatrical play—to engage him [or her] in a personal way."[32] Second, individuals are willing to pay more for experiences than for commodities, products, or services. Third, customization enhances experiences. This does not mean simply offering customers more choices, because, as Schwartz has revealed, having too many choices impedes decision making and creates frustrations for consumers.[33] The best experiences reveal customized options, based on participants' needs over time and within the context of the experience.[34] The streaming music service Spotify does this with its daily mix playlists, which are custom built for you each day based on the music you have most recently been listening to.

To illustrate these ideas, Pine and Gilmore provide a narrative that reframes thinking about the role of workers and the workplace, concluding that "work is theatre" wherein companies stage plays that engage customers.[35] In using this model, they are careful to note the pitfall of "equating experiences with entertainment."[36] They stress that "staging experiences is not about entertaining customers, it's about engaging them."[37] Indeed, it is! End users need to be engaged as actors in the unfolding narrative of the experience rather than simply remaining observers of it; they must become participants.

The same is true for employees. The authors of a Deloitte Insight trends report note, "High-performing companies have found ways to enrich the employee experience, leading to purposeful, productive, meaningful work."[38] This result is accomplished by expanding and redefining an employee's relationship with the employer. This approach assumes a more holistic view of life at work enabled by obtaining constant feedback from employees to monitor and take action to improve their ability to do their day-to-day work.

Too often efforts to create experiences result in customer service improvements, not the creation of an experience. Customers remain

audience members rather than actors in the production. Theater provides an entertaining representational illusion, whereas experiences within the experience economy should produce authentic, participatory engagement. Theater is produced through enacting a static script, but an experience is serendipitously co-created by the experience stager and participants, resulting in unique experiences each time. These are important differences in both production and result. Knowing this and its implications for experience design puts you ahead of many who are attempting to design experiences.

Let us provide you with a quick example of theater as a co-created experience. Mat once attended an immersive dance theater performance entitled *Sonder* directed by his friend and dance professor Graham Brown. Instead of taking place in a traditional theater setting, *Sonder* was staged throughout a three-story historic building. The performers enacted the show's narrative throughout the building, and participants were encouraged to wander freely. This meant that different scenes were happening simultaneously throughout the building. To add to the complexity and co-created nature of the experience, performers often interacted directly with audience members and pulled them into the action. For example, at one point a main character asked an audience member to babysit his daughter so that he and his wife could go to a party. The unique nature of *Sonder* transformed a traditional theater-as-entertainment experience into a theater-as-immersive experience.

Business Dictionary defines *production* as "processes and methods used to transform tangible inputs (raw materials, semi-finished goods, subassemblies) and intangible inputs (ideas, information, knowledge) into goods or services."[39] To this list we need to add experiences. The addition of experience introduces the question of whether experiences are produced in a similar manner to goods and services. We don't think they are. Producing experience is a new paradigm of production because of the requirement for co-creation with participants. Using theater arts vernacular, we often call it "staging" to confirm that it is unique from other types of production.

The notion that producing experiences is simply an extension of normal production processes is naively replete in the literature, and no one is suggesting otherwise. What is missing is an understanding of how experiences for individuals are produced. John R. Kelly states, "The leisure experience [and, we add, experience in general] is never

just receptive, passive. It is an involving process in which the players are all acting in one way or another."[40] It is produced one episode at a time by the people participating in the experience. In providing a service, where something is done to or for someone, control of production remains with the producer. Producing experience, however, requires a different paradigm of production, one in which the producer partners with the participant to co-create the experience. Remember, participants are actors in this drama.

This point was made clearer to Bob in spring 2018 when he and his wife took their two grandchildren to a dude ranch in Arizona. They had visited the dude ranch eight years earlier with their other two grandchildren. For their previous trip they had purchased western gear, including boots, cowboy hats, and clothes, to wear at the ranch. Most of the other guests during their initial ranch visit also wore western gear. But this time the experience felt different. Although the activities (e.g., horseback riding, skeet shooting) were still western themed, fewer guests wore western garb, opting instead for canvas shoes, tee shirts, and baseball caps. Since many of the guests did not play their part in this unfolding western drama, the experience seemed less authentic. Experience designers need to be aware of the role they want participants to play and clearly communicate these expectations.

Comparing experience staging to theatrical staging may create some operational misconceptions. For example, theater arts include set design, costume design, lighting design, being a playwright or perhaps a director. But all these are focused on producing something for a participant to spectate, not to participate in. The analogy with experience design is complete only if you think of participants as the actors who have a partial script and thus to varying degrees participate in determining interactions and outcomes.

Ultimately, the participant is a partner with the experience designer when the experience is staged, and this role needs to be anticipated and accommodated in the experience design. Compared to service production, experience staging is a more complicated and risky process. When a designed experience is staged, the designer does not remain in complete control of the production process because participants also play an active role. They are actors who can improvise the script as the event unfolds. A service is delivered in real time; an experience is co-created in real time.

Summary: Is It Worth It?

You may be thinking, "So, to design quality experiences I have to engage people's attention and meet their most important needs? This sounds complicated." Well, it is, sort of. It does require a systematic, intentional approach and an understanding of the social psychology of experiences reviewed in this chapter. You can't simply throw an experience together and have it consistently produce results of importance to you and your participants. Too often experiences are cobbled together as the experience is produced with no intentional planning. Luckily, this book is dedicated to providing you with a set of tools to intentionally and effectively design great experiences.

People want and need great experiences, but to provide them you have to design experiences that can capture people's attention. Research from a variety of disciplines gives some excellent insights into what makes a great experience. Such an experience includes our innate need for the right amount of stimulus—not too little and not too much. We also need to feel autonomous, competent, and connected to people around us. We want to experience things that elicit positive emotions, build relationships, develop skills, connect us to desirable networks of ideas and people larger than ourselves, and provide us with a sense of meaning and purpose. Everyone is looking for these types of experiences. Are you ready to design them?

In the next chapter you'll learn that experience is an expansive concept used to describe many different engagements. To put this in perspective, we have developed a framework that identifies the causal elements and resultant outcomes of different types of experiences. This framework will enable you to design macroexperiences that include intentional sequences of different types of experiences to produce your intentionally targeted outcomes.

CHAPTER THREE

A Framework of Experience Types

HOW WOULD YOU categorize the different experiences you have each day? Some are mundane, like taking out the trash; others are more memorable, like attending a special dining event where you eat your food in complete darkness, thus narrowing the sensory experience down to taste and smell. While all experiences share some common characteristics (e.g., multiple phased, requiring attention, based on perceptions), unique qualities distinguish certain experiences from others. In this chapter, we introduce a framework of experience types to help you differentiate between and intentionally design them. Before we get to the framework, though, we need to discuss briefly the important connection between consciousness and experiences.

The philosopher George Berkeley purportedly was the first to pose the question, "If a tree in a forest falls and no one is around to hear it, does it make a sound?" According to quantum mechanics, it doesn't. The authors of a 2018 *Scientific American* article entitled "Coming

to Grips with Quantum Mechanics" make the following claim about perceived reality:

> According to QM [quantum mechanics], the world exists only as a cloud of simultaneous, overlapping possibilities—technically called a "superposition"—until an observation brings one of these possibilities into focus in the form of definite objects and events. This transition is technically called a "measurement." One of the keys to our argument for a mental world is the contention that only conscious observers can perform measurements.[1]

When observers become conscious of an object or event, they "measure" or take note of it; thus, for something to exist it must be consciously measured, or it doesn't exist. To further support their argument, the authors quote the German theoretical physicist Max Planck, who said: "I regard consciousness as fundamental. I regard matter as derivative from consciousness. We cannot get behind consciousness."[2] Becoming aware of or being conscious of an object or event is its origin. It is interesting that this notion is also a fundamental tenet of the sociological theory of symbolic interaction—namely, that the meaning of objects derives from our interactions with them.

Thus, consciousness and the interactions inherent to achieving it are fundamental to understanding how we relate to the world we know. In the previous chapter we cited a number of social psychologists who have studied consciousness, also called "awareness" and "attention directing." Although consciousness is fundamental, there are varying degrees of consciousness; these varying degrees of attention and resulting variations of engagement with objects and events influence the intensity of the resulting experience. This variation provides a continuum of consciousness that is the underlying structure for the experience framework we present in this chapter.

The Framework

Our framework consists of the following five experience types: prosaic, mindful, memorable, meaningful, and transformational. Types are defined by their key characteristic as well as by the five attributes that form a continuum across the framework. Starting with experiences

that are mindful, the key characteristics are cumulative; in other words, they build on each other as you move across types. For example, the key characteristic of memorable experiences, emotion, is also found in meaningful experiences along with its unique characteristic, discovery. In presenting each experience type, we'll first identify its name, define its key characteristic, and then discuss the attributes that determine the experience type's placement within the framework.

Prosaic Experiences

Unless you have abilities of observation and memory recall like Sherlock Holmes, you probably don't remember the color of the toothbrush you had three years ago. This lack of recall is not because you didn't have adequate opportunities to interact with your toothbrush and memorize its color. You had been using it several times a day, we hope, for multiple months. The real issue is that the experience of brushing your teeth is routine and forgettable. Your brain goes into autopilot as you move through your familiar teeth-brushing routine, and you don't take the time to think, "Wow, my toothbrush is orange with white stripes down the side. I'm going to remember this toothbrush forever."

John Dewey, the renowned psychologist and educational reformer, described these types of occurrences as "prosaic experiences."[3] *Merriam-Webster* defines *prosaic* as "everyday, ordinary."[4] Most of the experiences we have each day are prosaic. They happen in Daniel Kahneman's system 1 thinking.[5] And guess what? That's okay; in fact, it's a good thing. Just think, if every experience you had each day required your full attention and stimulated every sense, you'd be exhausted before even leaving your house for work. Kahneman documents that our brains are lazy and reluctant to invest more effort than necessary;[6] that's why they shift into autopilot during prosaic experiences. This autopilot mode is the key characteristic of prosaic experiences.

As an experience designer, you need to recognize the importance of intentionally designing prosaic experiences. These experiences are a necessary part of an experience journey but not ones you design for participants to remember. In fact, well-designed prosaic experiences help end users avoid negative memorable experiences because they eliminate touchpoints that consume mental energy unnecessarily. For example, when Mat visits his dentist, he parks in an attached

parking structure adjacent to the building where the dentist's office is located. Recognizing that it's easy to lose track of which parking level corresponds to the office's building level, especially for patrons who visit the office only once or twice a year, Mat's dentist has placed signs on each level of the parking structure to guide patrons up to the correct level. This simple intervention ensures that the parking experience becomes prosaic after the first visit as opposed to becoming a negative memorable one at each six-month checkup. Although parking has nothing to do with dentistry, it has everything to do with the dental patron experience.

Mindful Experiences

Prosaic experiences become mindful experiences when they cause us to shift out of mental autopilot mode and engage in effortful mental activity. In doing this we shift from fast (system 1) to slow (system 2) thinking.[7] Dewey explained that the difference between mindful experiences and prosaic experiences is that during a mindful experience something catches our attention and cues our brain to shift out of autopilot to figure out what's going on.[8] Kahneman's work indicates that a function of system 1 activity is to assess what is going on in one's environment and determine if there is a need to shift to system 2 thinking.[9] The act of effortful thinking may be momentary or sustained; but as soon you engage in slow thinking, you shift from a prosaic to a mindful experience. For example, you may be walking from the subway station to your office building, a path you take every day, when you notice that the sidewalk you usually take is blocked for construction. You must now think about alternate routes and select one. You have learned a new route to work. It may even be better than your habitual route!

Effortful mental activity, therefore, is the key characteristic of mindful experiences. You are no longer passively moving through a rote routine; you have moved into system 2 thinking. Producing a mindful experience requires, at a minimum, an interruption of a prosaic experience. You need to get people's attention if you want them to break from their habitual, prosaic response. Bill Nye the Science Guy introduced the notion of the ABCs of teaching: action before content.[10] Action is the norm-breaking, attention-getting device used to create a teachable moment.

Let's consider the case of the airline flight-safety briefing. How could you apply Bill Nye's approach and place action before content to turn this traditionally prosaic experience (we know most of you zone out during this part of the flight) into a mindful one? Any ideas? If you've flown enough, you've probably noticed creativity emerging in the flight-safety-briefing experience with some airlines. Southwest Airlines has used humor for quite a while to catch people's attention during their safety talks. More recently, several different airlines, including Delta, Air New Zealand, and Virgin America, have produced some clever and humorous videos designed to catch people's attention in order to entertain and inform.[11] If effortful mental activity occurs, an experience is no longer prosaic. You may also think further or more intently and *feel* emotional intensity as you engage in system 2 thinking, thereby transitioning a mindful experience into something else entirely.

Memorable Experiences

We're going to ask you to engage in a short exercise. Take out a pen or pencil and list ten of your most memorable experiences in the space provided in this section. If you are one of those people who like to keep their books undefiled, you can use a separate sheet of paper.

1. ______________________________
2. ______________________________
3. ______________________________
4. ______________________________
5. ______________________________
6. ______________________________
7. ______________________________
8. ______________________________
9. ______________________________
10. ______________________________

What makes these experiences stand out in your memory? Do they share a commonality? Mindful that you can probably think of a variety of answers to these questions, we'd like to suggest that emotions are a key characteristic of all memorable experiences. If you look back at your list, you can probably distinctly remember the emotions involved with each one.

Emotions change mindful experiences into memorable ones. Consider the following example: As a river guide, Mat floated the same sections of the rivers he worked on numerous times. Because of the repetition involved, he does not remember the specific details of each trip, but he can recall experiences on the river associated with emotions: the thrill of running a particularly technical section for the first time, fear when a boat flipped or someone fell out during a rapid, contentment sitting around the campfire with a particularly tight-knit group of guests. Experiences on the river that didn't produce emotions have faded into the background.

The connection between emotions and memories is also supported by the work of Kahneman and his colleagues. Their work suggests that we remember experiences in the moment and after they occur differently.[12] Even though we evaluate an experience moment to moment as it's occurring, when we reflect on an experience we tend to remember peaks, pits, and ends of experiences.[13] This principle is often referred to as the "peak end rule." Those moments of the experience that produce the strongest emotions also produce the strongest memories. This is why Dan and Chip Heath argue that "you do not need to obsess over every detail" of an experience as long as you incorporate memorable peaks and ends.[14]

Although you usually want to design experiences that elicit positive emotions, you also need to have strategies in place to address negative emotions when they occur. As an experience designer, you must manipulate cues to facilitate the recall of positive emotions and memories. But you must also make certain the cues do not lead to the recall of negative memories. For example, Disney theme parks have an intentional plan in place for instances when a child gets lost.[15] The plan involves the coordinated efforts of cast members across the park as well as a lost-child center with books, games, and videos to occupy children until their parents are located. Cast members are trained to comfort and reassure both lost children and their parents. The parks have a very high success rate of quickly reuniting families, all without ever having to rely on making public lost-child announcements. They work intentionally with a predetermined plan to turn a negative experience into a positive one as quickly as possible by controlling the emotions of the child and parents, as well as by having a plan to quickly reunite them.

You can never fully design away bad experiences; they are going to happen. Part of an experience design process should include speculative forecasting about things that may go wrong and the response that will be provided if they do. This approach can be taken to unrealistic extremes, of course, but understanding human nature will lead you to a reasonable and probable list. Fortunately, experiences that initially produce negative emotions can serve as opportunities to proactively correct experience failures. Research even suggests that the best services often start as bad experiences that were then intentionally addressed and fixed by the provider.[16] You can probably think of personal examples of bad experiences transformed into good ones because an individual or organization took quick corrective actions and instituted a good recovery.

Meaningful Experiences

Memorable and meaningful experiences have a lot in common. System 2 thinking and emotions are common characteristics of each type. The key characteristic that differentiates a meaningful experience from a memorable one is discovery. Meaningful experiences teach us something about ourselves or expand our knowledge about the world. Look back at your list of ten memorable experiences. We wouldn't be surprised if they involved discovery of something new. Meaningful experiences are important because they serve as the building blocks of your personal identity and worldview. They represent times when we learn things that matter to us: a new insight about ourselves, a new fact we believe important, or a new insight about a previously held point of view.

Designing meaningful experiences is more difficult than designing the other experience types we've discussed so far. Meaningful experiences are often the result of co-creation in which participants play an active engaged role in the experience. Martin Seligman suggests that "we want to be entitled to our positive feelings."[17] In other words, we want to have played a part in acquiring positive feelings for our experiences to be truly meaningful. Co-creation facilitates this desire.

Participants also need time during an experience to reflect on the meaning of what has occurred and its personal implications. Our

professional experience suggests that this is further enhanced when individuals are given the opportunity to share memorable experiences with other people who are important to them and when the experience includes opportunities for personal reflection. When designing meaningful experiences, you should intentionally find ways to make them shared and provide space for individual and group reflection. You don't need to structure every moment of an experience with active engagements. Personal reflective engagements are engagements too! Remember our discussion in chapter 2 about autonomy as a basic psychological need. Sometimes the right amount of unstructured time, time for reflection about what has occurred, can enhance feelings of autonomy and move an experience from memorable to meaningful.

We should mention here that not all discovery, or learning, occurs as a result of meaningful experiences. Much, if not most, learning arises out of mindful experiences. Rote memorization of facts and figures seldom elicits emotion or discovery. Learning that sticks with you, though, that's a different story. Recall some of the most influential teachers in your life, and we wager they provided meaningful experiences ripe with emotion and discovery. In fact, they probably even provided you with transformational experiences as well.

Transformational Experiences

Over the course of your life, certain experiences will have a profound effect on the individual you are. These types of experiences are infrequent, and often we don't immediately recognize their profundity. This is because transformational experiences lead directly to personal changes born out of the experience. For example, an individual has a heart attack and, fortunately, survives. Because of this, that person experiences a shift in perspective about life and about attitudes regarding health and exercise. These attitudinal changes lead to dramatic behavioral adjustments related to the person's diet and exercise. Sustained over time, this behavior changes the person, who has thus become transformed because of the heart attack. It's important here to note that transformational experiences contain all the characteristics associated with the nonprosaic experience types reviewed thus far: reflection, emotion, and discovery. The new, key characteristic is significant change. Were any of the memorable experiences you noted on

your list transformational? If any of them led to perspective, attitude, or behavior changes, then they were.

It also deserves noting that within a transformational experience, there are usually one or two distinctly transformative microexperiences (remember the peak-end rule!) that make the entire macroexperience transformational. Consider Charles Dickens's timeless tale of the transformation of Ebenezer Scrooge.[18] His is a story of transformative encounters that cause Scrooge to dramatically change his behavior: seeing his younger self choose money over love with the Ghost of Christmas Past, or having the Ghost of Christmas Yet-to-Come show him Tiny Tim's family mourning Tim's passing. Because of his ghostly peak experiences, he proclaims, "I will honour Christmas in my heart, and try to keep it all the year. I will live in the Past, the Present, and the Future. The Spirits of all Three shall strive within me. I will not shut out the lessons that they teach!"[19] Scrooge's experience is transformational because he becomes a new man, and as the narrator confirms, "Scrooge was better than his word. He did it all, and infinitely more."[20]

Transformational experiences also vary by degree according to the type and duration of the change. Consider, for example, a hypothetical story of different individuals who watched the same TED Talk about nutrition. One person experiences a shift in her attitude regarding the consumption of processed foods but not enough to change her behavior. Another person has an attitude change about his nutrition and decides to give up sugar—but the resolution lasts for only one week. A third person who watches the TED Talk has a more lasting transformational experience that sets her on a path to becoming a professional triathlete.

Summarizing the Experience Types

The framework consists of five experience types and their associated key characteristics: prosaic (autopilot), mindful (effortful mental engagement), memorable (emotion), meaningful (discovery), and transformational (change) (see figure 3.1). Each characteristic, starting with effortful mental engagement, provides a foundation for subsequent higher-order experiences. Going forward, we'll refer to memorable, meaningful, and transformational experiences as "higher-order experiences" because they require additional personal investment when compared with prosaic and mindful experiences.

Prosaic	Mindful	Memorable	Meaningful	Transformational
Autopilot	Effortful Mental Engagement	Emotion	Discovery	Change

Figure 3.1 Experience types and key characteristics.

Experience Attributes

Five attributes determine the order of experience types within the framework. These attributes also help indicate differences between experiences (e.g., somewhat memorable versus very memorable) within specific types. The attributes are frequency and impact, novelty, engagement, required energy, and results.

Attribute 1: Frequency and Impact

During your lifetime, you will experience exponentially more prosaic than transformational experiences. In fact, the frequency of experiences decreases as you move from left to right across the framework. As Jenkins Lloyd Jones put it, "Life is like an old-time rail journey—delays, sidetracks, smoke, dust, cinders, and jolts, interspersed only occasionally by beautiful vistas and thrilling bursts of speed."[21] We all know that we are going to have a greater number of forgettable experiences than life-altering ones, but when it comes to experience design, too often the aspiration is that all experiences be transformational.

We believe that it's a bit unrealistic, as well as ineffective, to aim to design only transformational experiences. It's okay to design meaningful, memorable, mindful, and, yes, even prosaic experiences. People don't always want transformational experiences. When you go grocery shopping, you're not expecting or even desiring to have a life-changing experience. You want the process to be filled primarily with smooth prosaic and mindful experiences, perhaps with a few memorable ones thrown in for good measure. A master experience designer knows how to weave all experience types together to create a well-composed, positive macroexperience that meets or exceeds participants' expectations.

It is important to also note the inverse relationship of frequency and impact (see figure 3.2). It's the less frequent experiences that have the greatest potential effect, both negative and positive. As we move across

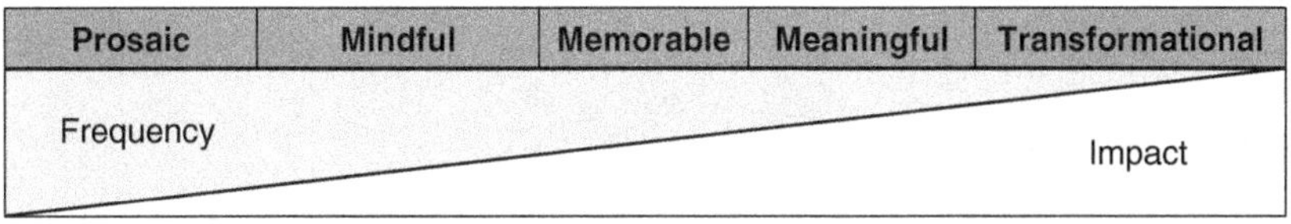

Figure 3.2 Experience frequencies and impacts.

the framework, the potential effect of experience results increases. In fact, the nature of potential results changes as well, which is a topic we'll address a bit later in the chapter.

As an experience designer, you need to recognize that the stakes increase as you create higher-order experiences. The payoff, in terms of results, of a well-designed prosaic experience is much less than the effect of a meaningful, memorable, or transformational one. At the same time, the potential for higher-magnitude negative experience results also increases as you move from left to right across the framework. In this regard, experience design can be compared to walking an inclined tightrope, with each experience type representing an increase in the height of the rope above the ground: greater risk, greater reward. Higher-order experiences require increased levels of participant buy-in. If you think back to the key characteristics, you can see that by the time someone has a transformational experience, that person has invested attention, emotions, identity, attitudes, and behaviors into the experience.

These investments are more likely to occur when participants co-create the experience with the provider, a topic we'll devote more attention to later. One-time or nonparticipatory experiences do not usually lead to repeat engagement or to the development of lifetime pursuits. These types of experiences are usually not engaging enough to produce long-term effects or participation; they are not sustainable. This doesn't mean that entertainment and one-time events can't produce high levels of engagement, but accomplishing these levels requires special design attention to create higher-order experiences in which participants become engaged actors as opposed to passive spectators.

Attribute 2: Novelty

The degree of novelty is obviously closely linked with frequency. Prosaic experiences are usually less novel than transformational ones

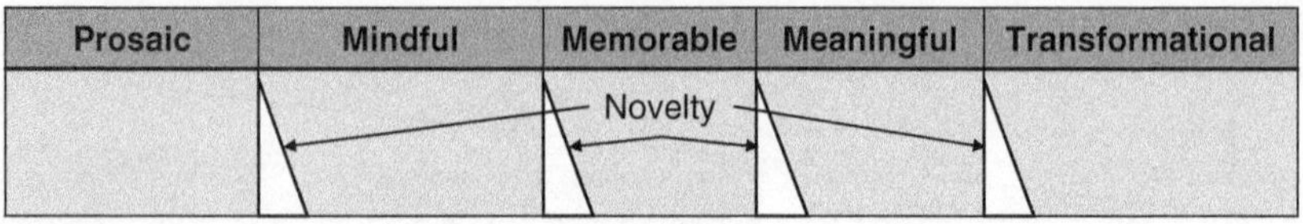

Figure 3.3 Experience novelty.

(see figure 3.3). The more we experience something, the less we tend to pay attention to it (i.e., we employ system 1 thinking). This is why experiences can change types over time with repeated participation. Novelty plays a key role in determining where experiences fall within the framework because its introduction encourages system 2 thinking. A little bit of novelty infused into even a prosaic experience can transform it into a different type of experience. Let's return to our earlier teeth-brushing example. Imagine you receive a fancy electric toothbrush. The usually prosaic experience of brushing your teeth now becomes mindful and perhaps even memorable. Teeth-brushing is suddenly novel and fun. Well, at least for a while. Novelty allows you to attract individuals' attention but the experience their attention is directed towards must also provide opportunities to feel, learn, and/or change or they will quickly lose interest. Novelty always has a point of diminishing return.

Michael Eysenck coined the term *hedonic treadmill*, based on thinking that goes back hundreds of years, to describe the process whereby individuals return to a baseline psychological state after positive or negative experiences occur in their lives.[22] A classic hedonic treadmill example is the effect of winning the lottery. In a study published in the *Journal of Personality and Social Psychology*, researchers found that lottery winners in their sample were not significantly happier than nonwinners.[23] Although winning the lottery is very exciting initially, winners tend to return to their previous level of happiness after the novelty wears off.

Although novelty can be an important tool for experience designers, it works only when applied sparingly and complimented by well-designed experiences. As Steve Diller, Nathan Shedroff, and Darrel Rhea note, "For companies to achieve enduring competitive advantage through experience design, their innovations cannot be based simply on novelty."[24] If you rely solely on novelty to engage people in

the experiences you design, you will be caught on the hedonic treadmill yourself, always having to find new ways to infuse novelty into your experience designs. Event designers often fall into this trap. They use a "wow" factor to end an event, which forces the need to create an even bigger "wow" for the next event. Novelty can be a useful experience design strategy, but it should be used judiciously and holistically.

Attribute 3: Engagement

Each experience type requires a different degree of participant engagement. Because the concept of engagement is abstract, we want to introduce some theoretical perspectives that should help you think more concretely about engagement. The first perspective is symbolic interaction theory, which was first developed by Herbert Blumer, based on the work of George Herbert Mead and others.[25] The basic idea of symbolic interactionism is that we assign meaning to the world around us as we interact with it. In other words, things have no specific meaning until we give them meaning through our interactions with them. Think of the logo of your favorite sports team. Now think of the logo of your favorite team's rival. The meanings you associate with each logo are built on interactions (i.e., experiences) you have had with those teams. The logos themselves are meaningless, but for fans of those teams they symbolically represent a host of experiences, emotions, and behaviors. This is symbolic interactionism in action.

What does this have to do with experience design? In a previous book, Bob and his coauthor Barbara Schlatter introduced a three-phase model (see figure 3.4), based on symbolic interaction theory, to describe how individuals engage in experiences.[26] During intake, the first phase, individuals become consciously aware of what is occurring in the experience. In phase 2, individuals begin to think more actively about the experience, process what is occurring, and may plan various options for responding. In the third and final phase, individuals respond and engage in co-creative actions that help sustain the experience. When individuals enter this third phase, they truly become participants. They introduce new touchpoints and elements that sustain interactions. Once the interactions introduced are resolved, conscious attention may shift back to the intake phase, thus beginning the cycle anew. Some experiences move participants through all

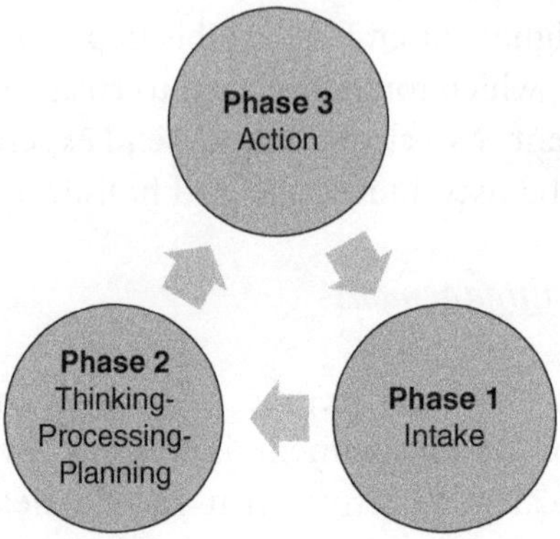

Figure 3.4 Action cycle. Reprinted with Permission. J. Robert Rossman and Barbara E. Schlatter, *Recreation Programming: Designing and Staging Leisure Experiences*, 7th ed. (Urbana, IL: Sagamore, 2015), 29.

three phases, whereas others may not even bring people into phase 1. Experiences with high affordance, which present multiple options for engagement, are more likely to be sustained, higher-order experiences. This is another way of modeling the difference between a service and an engaged experience. A service ends at phase 2 because participants are not provided options for engaging in and sustaining the experience.[27]

Have you ever fallen asleep in a movie? If so, you know what it's like when an experience can't even keep you in phase 1 engagement. On the other hand, have you ever watched a movie that has captivated you to the point where you have considered engaging in new behaviors (i.e., phase 3)? It's easy to recognize the effect of movies that facilitate phase 3 engagement. Take, for example, the behavior trends associated with the following movies:

- *Back to the Future*—increases in skateboard sales
- *Twilight* series—increases in vampire-teeth dental implants
- *Hunger Games* series—increases in archery participation
- *Sideways*—increased interest in pinot noir wine

Another example: each year millions of people attend Comic Con events all over the world to dress up and engage in activities associated with their favorite movies. This is indicative of phase 3 engagement.

Some definite parallels exist between the three-phase engagement model and Kahneman's system 1 and system 2 thinking. Phase 1 engagement is indicative of system 1 thinking, in which mental functioning is primarily on autopilot and reflection or deep thinking is limited. As you move into phase 2 and phase 3 levels of engagement, you also shift into system 2 thinking, which involves more intentional mental processes. Accordingly, higher levels of engagement and thinking are also associated with higher-order experiences (see figure 3.5).

Receiving a service provision, engaging in most entertainment offerings, and being a spectator are experiences that often end at phase 2 because no response from the recipient, audience, or spectator is required or allowed. These experiences are essentially passive. While this is fine some of the time, people also want phase 3 experiences in their lives. As companies have increasingly realized the importance of providing well-designed experiences, consumers' expectations for great experiences have increased. The world-famous Harlem Globetrotters realize this. Their main offering is a passive spectated show. However, they now offer a preperformance attraction marketed as the Magic Pass©: "Score more fun when you upgrade your game experience with Magic Pass presented by Tum-e Yummies, a 30-minute interactive event!"[28]

It is often the case that phase 1 and phase 2 experiences don't suffice. Richard Florida, writing about creative, well-educated individuals in *The Rise of the Creative Class*, comments, "They crave creative stimulation but not escape [;] . . . members of the Creative Class prefer

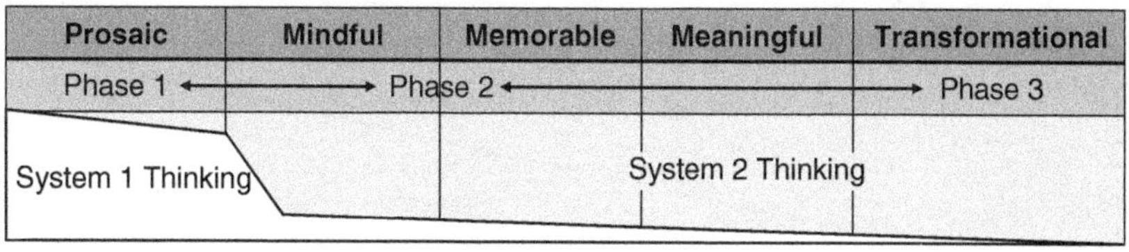

Figure 3.5 Experience engagement.

more active, authentic, and participatory experiences, which they can have a hand in structuring."[29] Sounds like they want to engage in co-creative experiences!

Attribute 4: Required Energy

Listening to advertisements today, you would think that higher-order experiences are widely available. Advertisers entice us with wonderful experiences of all kinds: purchasing experiences, ownership experiences, car service experiences, travel experiences, dining experiences, and so on. This barrage can make consumers feel that if they aren't having one amazing experience after another, they're missing out. And it can make an experience designer feel as if every microexperience needs to be an amazing, higher-order experience. This attitude, from both the participant and the designer perspective, is an illusion. You don't need to have or deliver a constant stream of higher-order experiences. A steady diet of higher-order experiences would be exhausting because these experiences require significant amounts of emotional and mental energy, both of which are exhaustible resources (see figure 3.6).

Every experience has an emotional, mental, and physical price tag, the "cost" of participating in the experience. Think of recent higher-order experiences you have had. We guess they required more personal energy investment than prosaic or mindful experiences. Often after a higher-order experience you need downtime to process what just happened. If you were to participate in one higher-order experiences after another, you would never have time for processing.

In some of his research, Mat has looked at the effect study abroad experiences have on adolescents.[30] Spending time internationally—interacting with foreign cultures and having a host of new experiences—is often

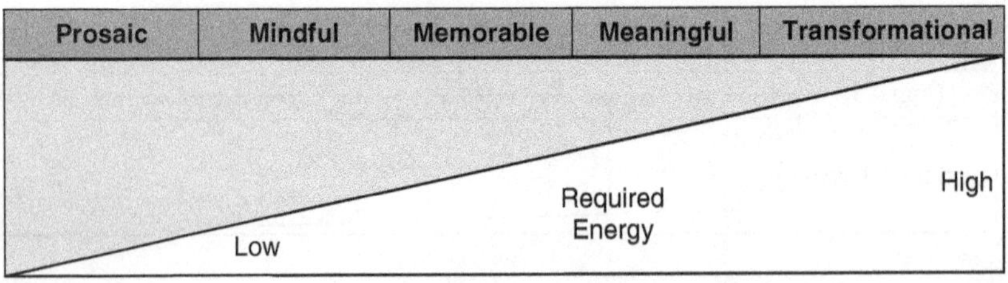

Figure 3.6 Energy required across experience types.

a memorable, meaningful, and even transformational experience. It is interesting that some participants in Mat's research expressed a desire for more time to reflect on the experiences they were having. Sometimes, in an effort to experience as much as possible during their travels, the interviewed students appeared to lose the ability to adequately process their experiences, and thereby they potentially missed out on recognizing the full effect these experiences had on their lives. This kind of disconnect might keep a memorable experience from becoming a meaningful one because time isn't provided for reflective discovery.

As we have already discussed, higher-order experiences happen only when individuals recognize and intentionally engage in what is happening around them. In her book *The Managed Heart*, Arlie Hochschild proposes a concept she calls "emotional labor," defined as "the management of feeling to create a publicly observable facial and bodily display; emotional labor is sold for a wage and therefore has an exchange value."[31] Hochschild goes on to suggest that "there is a cost to emotional work: it affects the degree to which we listen to feeling and sometimes our very capacity to feel."[32]

Experience designers need to recognize that some experiences require more energy than others and that some restore energy. Lessons along this line can be gleaned from the organizational behavior literature's recent interest in energy management. Although Steven Covey and others kicked off the time management movement decades ago, a growing awareness exists of the need for not only time management but also energy management. In a 2007 *Harvard Business Review* article titled "Manage Your Energy, Not Your Time," Tony Schwartz and Catherine McCarthy share the following advice to organizations that are attempting to maximize the effectiveness of their workforce:

> To effectively re-energize their workforces, organizations need to shift their emphasis from getting more out of people to investing more in them, so they are motivated—and able—to bring more of themselves to work every day. To recharge themselves, individuals need to recognize the costs of energy-depleting behaviors and then take responsibility for changing them, regardless of the circumstances they're facing.[33]

Schwartz and McCarthy go on to share data from studies they have conducted at large organizations, data that show a positive link

between effective employee energy management practices (e.g., better sleep patterns, healthy eating, short breaks) and increases in employee-generated revenue.

Be aware of the energy requirements of the experiences you design. In the same way a composer uses various tempos, tones, and instruments to create a symphony, the best experience designers employ a variety of microexperience types within the macroexperiences they design for participants. You have multiple keys on your experience design keyboard; make sure you use them all.

Attribute 5: Results

As previously noted, good experience design requires intentionally targeting specific results. To do this, you need to know what types of results you want your experiences to produce, types we hope have been derived from what your targeted participants need and want. It is equally important to understand the link between experience types and results. Too often, unrealistic claims are made about the results associated with the experiences provided. Do not fall into the trap of becoming an experience design snake-oil salesperson. David Meerman Scott argues that individuals want honest, fact-based information about what you offer, not an "egocentric display."[34] If we overstate the nature of the results our experiences provide, we are setting up our end users for disappointment. We need to recognize the link between specific experience types and specific result types. The question then becomes, Which outcomes are associated with which experience types?

Martin E. P. Seligman's work offers a potential answer to this question. In his book *Authentic Happiness*, Seligman discusses the nuanced though extremely important difference between two categories of positive results that stem from experiences: pleasure and gratification. He describes pleasures as having "clear sensory and strong emotional components . . . [that] are evanescent, and they involve little, if any, thinking."[35] Gratifications, in contrast, arise when experiences "engage us fully, [when] we become immersed and absorbed in them, and we lose self-consciousness."[36] Consider, as a concrete example, the different results associated with eating a donut versus helping someone in need. The first experience, according to Seligman, would produce pleasure, and the second, gratification.

Seligman makes a further distinction between bodily pleasures and higher pleasures. Bodily pleasures "are immediate, come through the senses, and are momentary."[37] Higher pleasures share many features in common with bodily pleasures but, Seligman notes, are also "considerably more complex in what sets them off externally. They are more cognitive, and they are also more numerous and more varied than the bodily pleasures."[38] He further classifies higher pleasures by their degree of intensity from low intensity (e.g., comfort and harmony) to high intensity (e.g., rapture and euphoria).

Gratifications are a bit more difficult than pleasures to conceptually pin down. Seligman observes:

> When I press people about the positive emotion of pleasure we allegedly feel when serving coffee to the homeless, or reading Andrea Barrett, or playing bridge or rock climbing, it is quite elusive. . . . It is the total absorption, the suspension of consciousness, and the flow that the gratifications produce that defines liking these activities—not the presence of pleasure.[39]

Think about our discussion of flow theory in chapter 2, and think about the flow-inducing experiences you've had. Those are examples of times when you've experienced gratification.

Let's return to thinking about experience types and results. Seligman's ideas about pleasures and gratifications map very nicely onto the framework (see figure 3.7). As we've previously noted, higher-order experiences are built on the characteristics and attributes of their lower-order cousins. In other words, memorable experiences involve reflection and emotion, whereas meaningful experiences involve reflection, emotion, and discovery. We use the same cumulative logic when thinking about experience result types. Accordingly, we propose that all experience types can produce bodily pleasures. Higher pleasures,

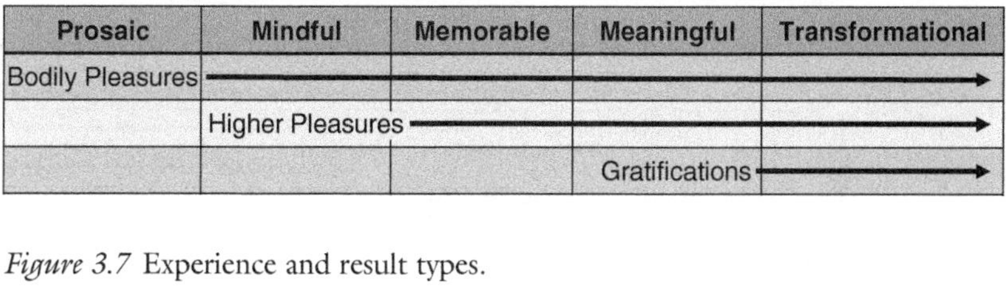

Figure 3.7 Experience and result types.

though, are associated only with mindful and higher-order experience types. Meaningful and transformative experiences are the sole domain of gratifications. Seligman further notes that

> [gratification] cannot be derived from bodily pleasure, nor is it a state that can be chemically induced or attained by any shortcuts. It can only be had by activity consonant with noble purpose. . . . The pleasures are about the senses and the emotions. The gratifications, in contrast, are about enacting personal strengths and virtues.[40]

Because gratifications are so closely linked with personal strengths and virtues, it's also important to recognize that these results are more likely to come about from active co-creation between designers and participants.

Framework + Attributes

So, there you have it. Five experience types and five attributes (see figure 3.8). We don't expect this framework in its current form to be the final word on experience types, but we at least hope to provide a usable, actionable framework to guide current practice and to promote further conversation. The experience type framework demonstrates

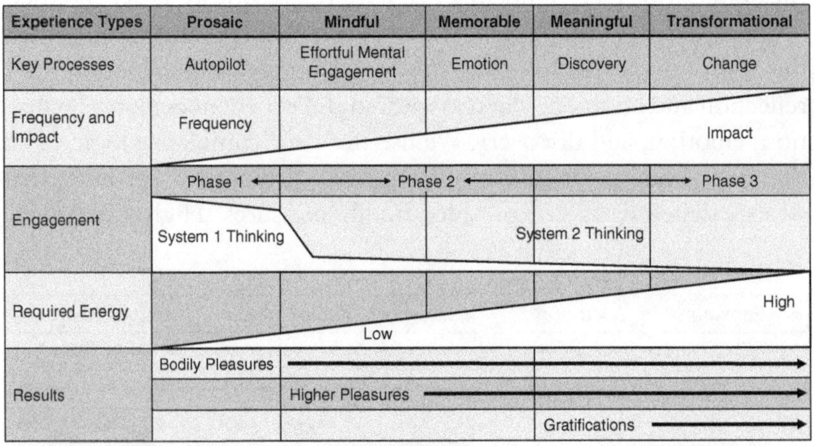

Figure 3.8 A framework of experience types.

the psychological underpinning to experiences that has not been fully explored and utilized in others' writings about experiences. We believe experience and experience design are better understood when anchored in this psychological literature.

The information included was further informed by our own work in designing experiences. The framework will help you develop a richer understanding of the nature of experience types and the things you need to consider when designing them. Each experience type is classified by its defining characteristic: prosaic, autopilot; mindful, effortful mental engagement; memorable, emotion; meaningful, discovery; and transformational, change. Lower-order experiences occur more frequently than higher-order experiences, but the potential magnitude of impact increases as you move from left to right across the framework. Novelty is most often a one-time, attention-getting bump that can initially capture individuals' awareness enough for a higher-order experience to occur if the experience also offers opportunities to feel, learn, and/or change. Higher-order experiences require more intense cognitive engagement (i.e., system 2 thinking and phase 2 reflective cognition and phase 3 intentional action). Because of these demands, higher-order experiences also require more energy. Finally, all experience types can produce bodily pleasures, whereas higher pleasures occur only in mindful and other higher-order experiences. Meaningful and transformational experiences are the domains of gratifications.

Before wrapping up this chapter, we want to provide an example of how the framework can help you classify, deconstruct, and design experiences. We also need to briefly discuss the role that time plays in all this. Let's first look at the framework in action.

Using a variety of experience types adds peaks and valleys. Let's return to the restaurant example we used in chapter 1, where we broke down the macroexperience into its microexperiences. We can use the framework to classify each of the microexperiences into one of the five types. This process allows you as an experience designer to have a much clearer picture and richer understanding of the macroexperience of visiting a restaurant. You can critically analyze the sequence, flow, and frequency of different experience types to better orchestrate the macroexperience. Perhaps you are devoting too many resources to making some microexperiences memorable when they should be simply prosaic. It is also possible there are microexperiences that could easily be moved from mindful to memorable.

When you identify a microexperience you want to shift from mindful to memorable, use the framework as a guide to make sure you're including the necessary characteristics and attributes of memorable experiences in your design. For example, you decide that you want to make the menu-reading experience more than just a chance to learn what's available and how much it costs. You could then brainstorm ways to make reading the menu a more emotional experience. Potential ideas include sprinkling tongue-in-cheek jokes throughout the menu to induce humor, adding riddles to produce feelings of accomplishment, or using a theme to connect readers to emotionally rich memories like holiday traditions or historical eras. In later chapters, we'll discuss in depth how to use design thinking to brainstorm and prototype new experience ideas and how to infuse artistic elements like themes into the design process. For now, we hope these examples of the framework in practice give you a sense of its utility.

Keep in mind that time can change one's perspective of experience types. The categorization of any experience you have is fluid because your perceptions of a completed experience can change over time. We've already noted that transformational experiences are often recognized as such not in the moment but later, after recognition of the resulting changes arises. Other experiences that may initially be memorable, meaningful, or even transformative may become prosaic over time with repetition. Consider your first day at a new job. It was probably a memorable experience—everything was new and exciting. As time went on and things became more routine, going to work each day became a mindful or prosaic experience.

It is interesting research shows that prosaic experiences can transform into higher-order experiences over time. Evidence for this was recently shown through a study conducted by Ting Zhang at Harvard in which participants wrote about some personal, yet ordinary life events.[41] Seven months later they read these descriptions again. Many of the participants were surprised at how meaningful these mundane reflections became over time. As one participant noted, "Re-reading this event of doing mundane stuff with my daughter has certainly brightened my day. I'm glad I chose that event to write about because of the incredible joy it gives me at this moment."[42] Mundane had become meaningful. The authors also note that the ease of recording and sharing immediate memories through social media may dampen this ripening effect because the focus becomes entirely on the act of

documenting, with little time given to reflection. They suggest that "future research should explore the optimal balance between enjoying the present as it unfolds and documenting the present to enjoy it in the future."[43]

Summary: Differentiating Experience Types

In this chapter we have moved from discussing experience broadly to discussing specific experience types. We have proposed and defined five types of experiences, each of which has different defining characteristics and attributes. The framework can help guide how you think about the different types of microexperiences you can use in composing each macroexperience. Paying attention to the details of each microexperience will help you to better orchestrate the overall macroexperience. We have also identified attributes associated with each experience type. You should think of these characteristics and attributes as possible ingredients for designing each specific type of experience. Knowing how various attributes contribute to each type and the degree to which they do so is useful for keeping design and staging efforts focused on delivering the intended microexperience to your end users. Next we turn our attention to the key elements of all experiences, the building blocks you will use to orchestrate experiences. These will be foundational elements for the experiences you will design.

PART TWO

The Experience Designer's Toolkit

ALTHOUGH THE TOPIC of experiences has received a lot of attention, how to go about systematically designing experiences deserves further examination. Our primary purpose in writing this book is to address this point. Much of the extant literature extolls the virtues of experiences and catalogues successful ones using case study examples. There is a process we have been developing for twenty-five years that can be used to intentionally design experiences. In this section we share it with you along with complementary content from top design-thinking and customer experience experts. This is a robust process that can be used to design new experiences or deconstruct existing experiences so that they can be improved. The following chapters introduce you to key topics you will need to understand in order to successfully design experiences: the experiencescape, design thinking, experience mapping, and touchpoint templates.

CHAPTER FOUR

The Experiencescape

WHEN MAT AND his wife, Chenae, were shopping for a house before moving to start a new job, their realtor sent them photos of a house in a desirable neighborhood. In the backyard of the house stood a large granite boulder that looked to be about six feet tall and six feet wide, a really large rock. Although the rest of the yard was overgrown and could not be clearly seen, both Mat and Chenae were intrigued by the thought of having a backyard with a large boulder as a signature piece their kids could climb and play on. They ended up buying this house and soon thereafter started the process of landscaping the backyard.

Although this was an exciting endeavor, it was also overwhelming. Neither Mat nor Chenae had landscape design expertise. They had a sense of what they wanted the yard to feel like, and both knew some basics about plants and trees, but they were aware that there was a lot about landscaping they knew little about. Luckily, they were referred to an up-and-coming landscape design student from the university who used his knowledge of the elements of landscaping to create an intentional and practical design for their yard. With this design in hand, Mat and Chenae could bring their hoped-for backyard to life,

with the granite boulder as a central feature (and, yes, their kids love playing on it).

Just as creating a backyard plan felt daunting to Mat and Chenae because they lacked an understanding of all the necessary elements of landscape design, so too can experience design seem intimidating without an understanding of the key elements of experiences. In chapter 1 we defined experiences (remember our discussion of micro- and macroexperiences?), but we didn't explain a critical aspect of experience design: the space in which experiences occur and the elements at play within this space. So, where do experiences occur? Although "everywhere" is technically correct, a designer needs more specificity. You could also answer, "They occur in individuals' minds," but though experiences are personally perceived, this also does not help you from a design standpoint. We like what Tom O'Dell has said about where experiences take place:

> The spaces in which experiences are staged and consumed can be likened to stylized landscapes: that are strategically planned, laid out and designed, . . . landscapes of experience—experiencescapes—that are not only organized by producers . . . but are also actively sought after by consumers.[1]

Notice the words O'Dell uses to describe the space where experiences occur: strategically planned, laid out, designed, and organized. All these words speak to the intentionality needed to create *experiencescapes*, a term Bob started using in the 1990s to help people to think more concretely about experience settings.[2]

In the same way a landscape architect intentionally arranges elements (e.g., irrigation, trees, shrubs, flowering plants, turf) to design landscapes, experience designers intentionally arrange key elements to create experiencescapes.[3] An experiencescape provides individuals with a structured environment in which they can engage in experiences. These six elements make up a "situated activity system,"[4] which is where the interactions of an experience occur. Think of the experiencescape as a stage and your participants as actors. You design the structure of the stage using its key elements (e.g., lighting, set pieces, backdrops, music), and then actors come onto the stage and interact with the structure in the space you have created and with each other. This interaction between the elements in this space and the actors in it is what creates

the experience. In this chapter we're going to introduce and explain how to use key experience elements to design experiencescapes.

In a previous book, Bob worked with Barbara Schlatter to identify six experience elements that have been used successfully for more than twenty-five years to design leisure experiences.[5] The work of other scholars interested in experiences has continued to confirm the applicability of the six elements.[6] We believe these elements, with a few adaptations, provide a starting point for defining the elements that are applicable across all experiencescapes. In the next section, we introduce our version of the six experiencescape elements and discuss their relevance for experience design.

Elements of the Experiencescape

Experiencescapes are composed of six experience elements: people, place, objects, rules, relationships, and blocking (see table 4.1 for more details). Each of these is unique and important—so important that if one is altered, the experience fundamentally changes. In every experience some elements are more important than others, but each element must be accounted for in an experience design. In some cases, one or more elements may be determined before the design process begins; for example, the *people* element may already have been determined (e.g., five-to-six-year-olds are the predetermined participants for kindergarten experiences). Although as a designer you must accept these givens, you can still create unique experiences through the modification of the remaining elements because modifying even one element can often profoundly change the overall experience.

People

People play a central role in all experiences. Recall our earlier discussion about conscious attention; experiences exist because people are conscious of them. If no one is aware of an experience, it doesn't actually happen. Because of the social bonding that can occur in experiences, you could also argue that if the right participants aren't part of the experience, you won't achieve the social outcomes that are possible. Delivering a successful experience directly depends on engaging the right people as participants.

TABLE 4.1
The Six Elements of the Experiencescape

Element	Description
People	All individuals involved in the experience, including participants and stagers, whether physically present or not
Place	The place in physical space and chronological time in which the experience occurs
Objects	Physical, social, and symbolic objects that play a recognized role in the experience
Rules	The rules that influence experiences, from codified laws to social expectations
Relationships	The relationships people in the experience share that influence their interactions
Blocking	The choreography of people's location and movement through an experience

Cruise lines, for example, understand this principle and try to clearly communicate the nature of their cruises. Some are family oriented and others are not. On their shore excursions, they clearly communicate the rigor of walking that is necessary to complete the trip. Children's toy manufacturers use a system to indicate the applicable age range for their toys and games to help parents ensure that they purchase age-appropriate items for their children. Covering all that would be useful to know about people is a large order, larger than we can cover in this book. Matching the right cohort of people to your experience and designing the experience for a specific cohort are the usual strategies.

We will get you started and motivated to know as much as practical and possible in this section. Understanding the people in your experiences is so crucial that we further develop techniques for accomplishing this understanding by discussing participant *personas* in chapter 6.

Knowing the motivations of the people participating in an experience is a good starting point to determine person-to-experience fit. What do your potential participants hope to get out of a particular experience? The answer to this question is usually apparent. People go to church for a religious experience. Many churches have expanded opportunities for congregants to participate in the service to provide a more authentic experience. So, if you know why people are coming to your experience, you have a better chance of fulfilling their desires

with an on-target experience design. But figuring out motivations is not always so simple. Individuals who participate in the same experience often have diverse motivations and report varying results.

A broad array of characteristics makes people different from each other. These include socioeconomic variables, gender, age, and ethnicity, to name a few. They also include performance variables such as the level of experience and skill individuals have with the experience in question. Experiences designed for experts will be much different than those designed for beginners.

We imagine that as you've read through this section, you've thought primarily about your potential participants. That's great, and they're important, but you need to think about all the people who will be involved in the staging of the experience. For example, a game of college football obviously includes players as the main participants, but coaches, referees, cheerleaders, event staff, spectators, and media members all have different roles to play. If you consider in advance how to design the roles these various individuals will play as part of the overall experience, the whole experience will be better for everyone involved. Frontline staff members are often a make-or-break element of an experience. Make sure that they know what is expected of them, they have the skills to complete expected tasks, and they have a clear understanding of how their actions will contribute to end users' experiences.

In addition, in some experiences individuals who are absent from the experience can influence the behavior of those present. For example, a vocalist's performance will be influenced by what her voice coach has previously taught her. Children will be influenced by what their parents have taught them. This category also includes the people providing the experience who are not physically present. Later in the book we will call these people "backstage contributors." The number involved can quickly become a large group when you consider all the people associated with delivering an experience, but some are more important than others. A bride's wedding dress designer plays a more salient role in the success of a wedding reception, for example, than the person who cut down the trees that were eventually fashioned into the backdrop trellis. At the same time, the best experience designers are aware of and consider the role that key behind-the-scenes, backstage contributors play in bringing experiences to life. In some cases, their roles form an interesting backstory that may add to the overall experience. This will be discussed further later in the book.

We hope we've convinced you of the importance of knowing all you can about the people who will play a part in your proposed experience. You need to use available resources to learn as much as possible about them. Too often, because of a lack of information, experience designers work from their own perspective rather than from the perspectives of those who will participate.

Place

Thomas Wendt, in his book *Design for Dasein*, discusses the German meaning of the word *Dasein*: *Da* means "here or there," and *Sein* means "being there."[7] He continues, "Dasein is situated Being."[8] So, the direct translation of his book title is *Designing for a Situated Instance of Interaction*. We believe that the six elements we are presenting situate *being* in time and space. They serve as the primary raw materials the experience designer uses to build a situated, structured experience. Place is one of these elements. The place an experience occupies matters. This includes both its chronological and its physical location, which situate the being or existence of the experience in time and space. It is interesting that current research on the physiology of the brain in accounting for and recording experiences has focused on these two elements, the space where an experience occurs as well as the time stamping the various encounters or touchpoints that compose the experience.[9]

A good example of the importance of chronological location is date-dependent experiences like holidays and birthdays. May Day is always May 1. Christmas is December 25. St. Patrick's Day is March 17. The experiences associated with the traditions and rituals of these days would not be the same on other dates. Although some people would rather forget their birthday, for others it's a celebration that can't be moved or made up for later. In some cases, experience designers try to piggyback on the aura of these special days by holding them at other times of the year. For better or worse, we get Christmas in July, half-birthday celebrations, and so on. But these experiences often feel like cheap knockoffs of the original.

Many experiences are dependent on the time of day. Easter sunrise services are obviously held when the sun comes up. A New Year's celebration comes at midnight in each time zone. Brunch bridges the time usually reserved for breakfast and lunch. While this all may seem

obvious, it's important to recognize that time is an important element in your experience design toolkit. Scheduling a program at a different or unusual time of day can add excitement and variety. Night golf, played with balls that glow in the dark, is a novel change from how and when the game is usually played. It is not enough fun to become the norm, but it is fun to do occasionally.

Let's now shift our focus to the physical location of an experience. The *venue*, a term we use to describe the physical setting in which an experience occurs, has a significant effect on an experience. Each venue will have facilitating and constraining elements. Some venues are iconic—Times Square on New Year's Eve, for instance. People experience a new year every year, but experiencing the new year in Times Square is a novel and memorable event for many. Other venues have no obvious meaningful associations. This allows experience designers to start with a blank slate.

When selecting a physical location, you need to think carefully about all the characteristics of a physical location that are discernable through the five senses: taste, smell, sight, touch, and hearing. Thinking intentionally about the sensory characteristics of your experience's location is extremely important because humans are hardwired to pay attention to and remember physical settings, especially those where important experiences occurred. Taste and smell are particularly powerful memory triggers.

Mat loves the scene in the Disney movie *Ratatouille* when the food critic Anton Ego comes to write a review of the protagonist's restaurant. He is served a seemingly uninspiring and provincial dish of ratatouille, but the taste of his first bite transports Anton back to the warmth, familiarity, and love of his mother's kitchen. In this moment, his meal in the restaurant becomes inextricably connected to cherished childhood memories, and so he later writes a glowing review. What do you want your experiences to taste and smell like? It's no coincidence that Main Street in Disneyland smells like waffle cones and freshly popped popcorn. These aromas are artificially diffused throughout this area of the park because they significantly contribute to the experience.

Sight is straightforward: What does the space look like? Is it clean? Does the visual layout of the physical space fit the experience? For some experiences, the designer will need to carefully plan to change the look and feel of a venue using decorations. Event planners, including wedding planners and other special-event planners, put great effort into flowers,

table arrangements, tableware, centerpieces, lighting, and other ways of altering a venue to make it contribute to the intended experience.

What does the space feel like to the touch? Bob used to ask his students to identify experiences in which touch played a primary role in recalling the experience. Students consistently identified two experiences. One was dancing at concerts. They loved the feeling of dancing in a tight crowd to the beat of the music. The second was spending time at the beach. They loved feeling the sand between their toes, the pleasant breeze of the moist ocean air on their skin, the feel of saltwater dried on their bodies, and the feel of the shower water that removed it. Touch matters, often in ways we do not expect.

What do you want your experience to sound like? This consideration includes both volume and types of sounds. Undoubtedly you've had experiences where sound levels were either too loud or too soft, and it's amazing how this one element can derail an otherwise great experience. Think carefully about what you want people to be hearing during different parts of the experience. If you expect people to talk with each other and you are playing music, make sure it's not too loud. If you want to drown out conversations, then play the music louder.

If you can get the elements of physical location right, you've got a good foundation for providing an excellent experience. In some cases (e.g., you're designing a product-driven experience), you may have little control over place. You may, however, be able to provide guidance about the best and least desirable places in which to use the product. Although some newer cell phones can be used almost anywhere, most small portable electronic products that plug in come with cautions about not using them while bathing or showering.

What we have pointed out in this section is straightforward but fundamentally important. If you change the place, you change the experience. Imagine hiking through a tropical rainforest contrasted with hiking through the mountains with a light snow falling. Both experiences involve hiking, but they are very different experiences, and the difference is in the setting. Simply put: place matters, a lot.

Objects

An object is anything that can have attention called to it and be acted on. This classification includes physical objects, social objects, and symbolic objects. Physical objects are obvious: you can see and touch

them. Social objects are other people. Symbolic objects are concepts or ideas that influence interactions within experiences. Patriotism, competitiveness, and religiosity are all symbolic objects that motivate us to act in specific ways.

In the game of basketball, objects from each of these categories influence interactions in the game. The ball, the backboard and basket, and the court are the primary physical objects. Secondary physical objects are the uniforms and shoes (and today's designer shoes have raised the ante about the importance of shoes). Teammates, members of the other team, your coach, referees, and fans are the primary social objects. Finally, the rules, the playing strategies the coach has taught, and the clock are the primary symbolic objects. Collectively, these objects govern the interactions within the game and both constrain and enable the overall quality of the experience.

In some sports, the focus is on the physical objects used in the game. For example, golf club and ball manufacturers compete fiercely to promote their products to golfers. In basketball, however, little attention is paid to the manufacturer of the ball, the hoop, the net, or the backboard. Because the game is usually played under the same rules, the focus of basketball is on the differential skills of the players and the unique game strategies devised by different coaches. In this setting, coaches are the experience designers of the players' experiences. They contribute to outcome by recruiting good players, preparing them physically, motivating them, and developing excellent game-playing strategies. Physical training techniques are well known and generally practiced similarly by most teams. Setting recruiting aside, a basketball coach's main contribution is providing players with unique strategies for playing the game and motivating them to win, both of which are symbolic objects.

Contrast this to auto racing, in which the outcome results from the interaction between the skill of drivers, the competence of their pit crew, and the performance of their automobiles. The top drivers have similar driving skills; and although there is some strategy regarding when in a race to make pit stops, this can change based on unanticipated wrecks on the racetrack that result in yellow caution periods. Vehicle performance accounts for a lot of the difference in outcome, which means that auto racing relies heavily on a primary physical object of the experience—the race car.

Our point is that the experience designer must know how these different types of objects contribute to and influence experiences.

This can become very important when anticipating and designing an experience involving a product. The product's manufacturer assumes that the product will be the focus and determiner of the experiences in which it will be used. But this may not be the case. Understanding the experiences the product will facilitate is critical to features of the product as well as to the marketing strategies developed to promote the product. You may have seen many ads for golf clubs and balls but none for basketballs, for example. In chapter 10 we will discuss in detail designing a product to facilitate an experience.

People play the role of social objects in experiences. Because they are capable of self-reflexive, mindful behavior, other people offer more interactive possibilities during an experience than any other object. You must take account of the other people involved in experiences, reflect on and interpret what they are communicating, and develop your own line of response to them depending on this interpretation. You are also influenced by people who are not present in the experience. Your behavior, how you respond to others, is to some degree guided by a range of social norms and conventions you have learned from your social network. These collective influences on our behavior have been called a "generalized other."[10] Everyone has a unique combination of these influences, though some are predictable. For example, Bob was once in China on a river cruise with a cohort of Americans. The last evening each national cohort was to sing a song. Bob's group decided to sing "Take Me Out to the Ball Game." The Chinese cruise director was not surprised. He told Bob that 95 percent of the American groups sing that song! Their singing it was predictable with almost complete certainty.

Another illustration of this "other" phenomenon is the concept of a team. Let's return to the basketball example used earlier. An individual player often makes plays and moves on the court in anticipation of where and how teammates will move. In this case, the team influences an individual's behavior. An experience designer must be aware of any such generalized others that may be present in an experience and anticipate their likely influences. For example, one Thanksgiving Bob's wife invited an exchange student from Holland to have dinner with their family. She asked Bob to pick up flowers for the dining table. Bob responded that it was almost certain a European would bring flowers as a hostess gift. Indeed, the young lady brought flowers for Bob's wife to the dinner.

Rules

Experiences are guided by a range of rules, from established laws to social mores. Their effects must be anticipated and incorporated into the design of an experience. In some cases, an experience designer may need to devise additional rules to increase the probability that an experiencescape will produce the intended type of experience and associated results. Let's examine the various levels of rules that may influence interactions in an experience.

The highest level of rules includes the laws of the nation, state, and local authorities. In most cases, it's reasonable to expect that individuals who come to your experience will know the laws. In some cases, however, the experience designer may need to remind people about specific laws that may affect an experience. For example, alcohol and smoking may not be allowed in certain venues. In international travel, it's often important to remind people of unique or different laws in countries they are visiting.

The second level of rules is social norms. There are numerous courtesies that govern our everyday interactions: greeting each other, queueing for service, taking turns in a classroom, or giving deference to older people and the disabled for seating. In today's multicultural society, experiences are often populated by diverse cohorts of people who may have disparate social norms. These and similar differences need to be anticipated and reconciled in an experience design before staging the experience.

A third level of rules involves those that may be unique to a specific experience. In games, for example, there is almost always a set of rules that governs how the game is played. In organized sports and other more formalized games, the rules almost always try to ensure that the winner has best demonstrated whatever is being contested. So, in basketball, the team with the most points has demonstrated that its players are superior in running, passing, rebounding, dribbling, and so on, all of which result in getting the best shots and the most points. Occasionally a team with less skill will win, but in most cases the team that best performs the relevant skills will claim victory.

When a team develops a strategy that seems to give its players an unfair advantage or an advantage inconsistent with the skills of the game, rules are often changed. In basketball, the University of North

Carolina coach Dean Smith developed the four-corner offense to slow down game play and reduce overall scoring. Players would assume positions, one in each corner of the offensive side of the court, with one player "floating" in the middle. They would simply keep passing the ball to each other with no movement toward the basket and no intention of scoring. In today's fast-paced game of basketball, this approach seems unfathomable. But the strategy of slowing down the flow of the game by possessing the ball for extended periods of time often kept opposing players with the most skill at shooting from scoring points and winning. The rules were changed by instituting a shot clock, which limited the amount of time a team could possess the ball on offense, thus negating the four-corner strategy.

In less formal games, like board games, there is almost always an interesting interplay between skill and luck that determines outcome. A luck mechanism is used because people of differing skill are playing the game, and the introduction of chance to partly influence outcome equalizes the possibility of any player winning. For example, the use of dice or spinning devices is intended to introduce chance in these games. These chance devices may be used to determine initial position or the number of advances a player may make. Snakes and Ladders, for example, is a table game whose outcome is fully dependent on chance. Thus, adults can play it with children and each player has a chance of winning, even the child. Winning at chess, in contrast, is almost fully dependent on skill. This mechanism of increasing chance as a determinant of outcome can often be used in an experience design to increase interest when people with unequal skill play together.

The fourth level of rules involves the social roles that individuals play out in an experience. A social role comprises a set of behaviors, rights, and obligations that come with a specific position. In formal situations, these roles are explicit. In basketball, coaches, players, referees, and spectators all have specific role expectations. Among the players themselves, forwards, guards, and centers each have specific roles (or expectations) to perform in various ways. At the venue where the game is being played, there will be ticket takers, ushers, medical first responders, and security personnel. The roles that these cohorts of people each play are well defined and different.

Roles still exist in less formal experiences, but they may not be as well defined. An important design decision is how much leeway to allow frontline employees as they perform their roles. Early in the

operation of Disneyland, all ride operators were given explicit instructions. The role they were to play with guests was well defined and usually scripted to contribute to the unique theme of the specific ride. The only exception was that guides on the Jungle Cruise ride could develop their own jokes and scripts. For this reason, Disney employees coveted Jungle Cruise jobs.

Tour leaders on guided tourist trips perform their roles to meet customer expectations. Tourists generally expect the leader to take care of them in unfamiliar surroundings, ensure a safe journey, guide them to the most significant sights, and share some knowledge about the sites to be visited. The pacing of these journeys and the amount of information provided often vary widely based on role performance choices made by tour leaders. In summary, rules play a big role in experiences. You need to be aware of relevant laws, social norms, and experience-specific rules and role expectations when designing experiencescapes.

Relationships

Experience designers must anticipate and account for pre-existing relationships that participants are likely to have and the potential influence these may exert on the experience. The three most common relationship arrangements include people already in relationships (e.g., friends and families), people with no existing relationships, and mixed groups where some people know each other but others don't.

The first question to settle is whether relationships have any bearing on the experience. Can people have the experience without interacting with their accompanying participants? This is often the case. The audience in a movie theater, for instance, is usually a mixed group, but there is no need for everyone to get to know each other before the movie starts. In other cases, like a wedding luncheon, relationships do matter, and they deserve specific design attention.

A second point to consider is whether the experience will be enhanced by participants getting to know each other. If so, the experience design will need to include mechanisms to facilitate this. For example, at sporting events, cohorts of family and friends often attend along with lots of people who don't know each other. The only relationship these diverse groups have with each other is that they are fans of a specific team. Usually the experience design mechanisms used in this situation are intended only to enhance the participants'

relationship as co-fans. Team colors, logos, fight songs, yells, and other such mechanisms are used to help these diverse individuals socialize as co-fans. Most often, there is no attempt to get them to socialize on any other dimension, and pre-existing cohorts can enjoy the experience on a parallel basis as family and friends and as co-fans.

If there is no need for people to get acquainted, to try to push this point is often counterproductive. These people have come with pre-existing family or friend cohorts, and forcing them to expand their group often comes at the expense of their desire to deepen their familial and friendship relationships. It would be rather awkward if you were asked to walk around and introduce yourself to everyone in a restaurant before ordering your meal. But in other situations, people need to get to know each other to fully engage in the experience. For example, in a multiday river-float trip, the rafts used will probably accommodate larger groups of people than the cohorts that have signed up for the trip. The groups on each raft need to get to know each other so that they can function as a team to paddle the rafts down the river and work together to complete camping duties each night. Thus, the guides will need to take specific steps, like icebreaker activities, to develop some sense of esprit de corps on their rafts.

Blocking

The final experiencescape element, blocking, involves structuring how people in the experience will move through chronological time and physical space. It is this motion through time and space and the affective role participants play in this motion that makes experience a unique human phenomenon.[11] Claude Romano, the French philosopher, states that "experience, in its fundamental sense, is that which, by putting us in play ourselves, modifies us profoundly in a way that *after* having crossed, endured, traversed it, we will *never* be the same again."[12] Wolff-Michael Roth and Alfredo Jornet, two science education writers, emphasize that experience is unique because it moves through time and space and involves affective interaction between participants.[13]

Envision a movie production set where all the five elements are in place and everyone is waiting for the director to yell "action." When "action" is shouted, the motion part of a motion picture begins. Until then, it is just a still photograph. The process by which a director determines where and how people move through the set is "blocking."

Experience designers must intentionally structure the blocking of an experience to influence the sequence and flow through time and space to put the experience in motion.

Let's examine another example, this time from an art museum. There are currently three methods used to move people through galleries. One is a self-guided tour enabling patrons to move through the gallery at their own speed and view whatever comes next or make their own choices about what to see using a printed guidebook. A second method is a preplanned audio tour that provides commentary about set pieces and has a strategy about which pieces will be pointed out for viewing. A third method is a guided tour with a docent or staff member. Usually these latter tours involve viewing fewer pieces but listening to more commentary about each piece. So, there you have it—three different experiences at an art museum, each differentiated from the others by how it is blocked.

Art museums as well as other types of museums are trying to deal with techniques for blocking that move a mostly spectator, observer experience into a participatory one. Nina Simon's book *The Participatory Museum* is a call to action for rethinking how people experience museums and cultural institutions.[14] She ponders: "How can cultural institutions reconnect with the public and demonstrate their value and relevance in contemporary life? I believe they can do this by inviting people to actively engage as cultural participants, not passive consumers."[15] The book includes many wonderful suggestions, all focused on creating opportunities to participate in experiences rather than simply being passive consumers. Science museums especially have taken on this charge to provide participatory experiences illustrating and teaching various scientific concepts.

Are there other methods of blocking? We have already identified one method: having an appointed leader. This is a time-honored method and probably the most used. Examples of appointed leaders include classroom teachers, preachers, sport coaches, football quarterbacks, theater directors, and tour guides. Because this approach requires employing people, it can be the most expensive blocking method. Many organizations now use docents and volunteers to lead in order to keep costs low. Having a designated leader is indeed a sure way to animate an experience. And, in some cases, the leader is the key element in the experience. People will pay a premium to attend a program on personal finance led by Dave Ramsey or Suze Orman.

Although many experiences are animated by leaders, not all leaders are the same, of course!

The pacing of an experience also is a component of blocking. You might remember the famous *I Love Lucy* candy factory episode, where the initially slow candy-production line suddenly speeds up and Lucy and Ethel cannot keep up. To avoid such a scenario in your designed experience, you need to make sure the pace promotes the desired experience. The pacing of a trip or tour for senior citizens or children affects participant enjoyment. Bob recently took a cruise where walking-tour groups were designated as fast paced or regular paced depending on the participants' ambulatory abilities. People could select which group to join. After the first day, several people moved groups based on the previous day's experience. In tour groups, also, the guide always experiences tension in whether to tell folks a lot about a few attractions or be briefer but cover more attractions. Some participants like a lot of information, whereas others want to see a greater variety of attractions.

Another method of blocking we have not yet discussed is mechanical. Amusement parks use this method to move individuals through their various attractions. Customers ride on some type of themed seating, such as a boat or airplane, and are moved along a track of some kind. In some ways this approach is akin to the Henry Ford assembly line. People ride on the assembly line and view various mechanical displays along the way, and what is produced is an experience. Some of these attractions do not allow much interaction by participants, although newer ones are incorporating interactive opportunities to make them more engaging and the experience provided more sustainable. For example, a number of Disneyland rides based on the *Toy Story* movie franchise, Buzz Lightyear's Space Ranger Spin and Toy Story Midway Mania, allow riders to shoot guns at targets. Individual rider scores are recorded and posted at the end of each ride, adding co-creative and competitive elements to the experience.

Time can also be used as a blocking device. A countdown clock is used in many sports and other gaming events to move an experience along. Many computer games and other virtual-reality experiences are moved forward in time by a countdown clock. The time constraint creates anticipation and excitement and also allows participants to know beforehand how long the experience will last.

Other mechanisms for implementing blocking include a printed self-guide booklet, signage providing a point-to-point path through an attraction, and the like. An experience designer must anticipate the need to block the experience and employ an appropriate method for doing so. Having the skill to visualize and vicariously participate in an experience is an essential tool experience designers require to effectively block an experience. We will discuss this topic more in chapter 7.

The Ubiquitous Web and Social Media

In today's world, the role of technology needs to be taken into account when designing an experience. Although we did not add technology as a seventh element, the ubiquity of technology like mobile devices and social media cannot be ignored. Potential participants will likely learn of your offered experience through some form of social media, they may sign up for it using their mobile device, and they will often evaluate it and communicate about their experience with their friends through social media. David Meerman Scott offers excellent advice about this topic in *The New Rules of Marketing & PR*. According to Scott, the web is the primary source of information for billions of individuals worldwide,[16] and their primary access device is their mobile phone.[17] He offers a number of tips useful to experience designers, including these:

- The web has provided access to small groups of potential niche customers not previously accessible.
- Web users are seeking information and knowledge, not hyperbole about your offerings.
- To be well positioned in the web, you must understand the keywords your buyers are using and use them in your copy.

The preceding list is derived from Scott's work.[18] His book not only explains the new rules but also teaches you how to deal with them to access potential customers of your experiences. Designing a great experience is critical, and we are teaching you how to do that. But you also need to market your experiences well to obtain actual consumers. Scott teaches you how to do that.

Summary: The Unending Variety of Experiencescape Combinations

All experiences occur in experiencescapes that are made up of six elements. These elements are fundamental; if you change one, you may change the entire experience. If you change the rules of a game, you have changed the game in some way. If you change the players in a game, you change game strategies, performance capabilities, and so on. These elements are the primary building blocks available to help you intentionally design an experiencescape and produce the experience you intend. Here we have also introduced the notion that you need to be able to market your experience over the web to succeed.

In many cases, the experience designer is given one or more elements and asked to manipulate the others to create an experience. For example, you may be given a specific product—an object to be acted on in an experience—and asked to design an experience or experiences to which the product could contribute. We discuss this in detail in chapter 10 with an example of developing the Golf Buddy© product for use in the golfing experience. You may have a venue—a fly-fishing camp, for example—and be asked to develop experiences that could be operated there to create revenue streams for the enterprise. The permutations are endless, but these elements provide a fundamental framework around which your design efforts will be organized. As we build your experience design skills, in succeeding chapters we will present a process for using these six elements to design experiences. In the next chapter we explain how the principles and processes of design thinking can be employed in experience design.

CHAPTER FIVE

Experience Design Thinking

IN CHAPTER 1 we quoted the following statement about what it means to design something: it is "the ability to imagine that-which-does-not-yet-exist, to make it appear in concrete form as a new, purposeful addition to the real world."[1] In this chapter we want to introduce you to a methodology, called "design thinking," that will help you infuse innovation into the design of your experiences. When you engage in experience design, though you often draw inspiration from other experiences, you are creating something new and unique. Venturing into the unknown with only creativity as a guide can energize some but paralyze others.

Many people view creativity as an ability endowed at birth. Either you're creative or you're not. This myth, along with many other talent-related myths, has been soundly disproved.[2] Although genetic and environmental factors influence innate differences in creative propensities, through volitional engagements of various experience design problems, you can develop your own creativity. In a similar way that muscles grow stronger with regular exercise, creative abilities develop when given frequent opportunities for application.

In *Creative Confidence*, Tom and David Kelly make an excellent case that anyone can increase the ability to engage in creative work.[3] Some people may seem more naturally creative, but it's most likely because they've spent more time engaged in creative activities. They have practiced being creative, which means they have probably had their fair share of creative failures as well, and that's okay. Too often, when it comes to creating something new, it's assumed that perfection is required on the first try. This is simply not true. Creativity is messy. A final, polished creative end product is almost always built on a foundation of imperfect previous efforts. This is true of almost every great artistic or scientific breakthrough. Consider the case of Thomas Edison, who definitely wasn't afraid of failure. He experienced thousands of unsuccessful attempts before inventing the incandescent light bulb. His failures paved the way to his eventual, world-changing invention.

We give you license to be imperfect when designing experiences. We hope you experience many failures along the way, as long as you keep moving forward. In fact, failing fast and frequently is a key principle of all creative acts, including experience design, because this is how you learn what's working and what needs further development.[4] To reap the benefits of failure, you must be willing to share your ideas before they're ready so that you can get frequent feedback early in the design process. In this chapter, we're going to show you how to employ a tested innovation process to tackle the wicked problem that is experience design.

Wicked Problems

Designing experiences is complex. As an experience designer, you have to situate the elements of the experiencescape in a way you think will produce desirable perceived results for participants, other key stakeholders, and yourself. There's a lot going on when you are designing an experience with the goal of producing intentionally targeted results for a specific group. This is what makes experience design a classic example of a wicked problem.

Horst Rittel and Melvin Webber's 1973 paper, "Dilemmas in a General Theory of Planning," brought attention to the concept of wicked problems.[5] In their paper, Rittel and Webber contrast tame and wicked problems. Tame problems are clearly defined and have clear

solutions. The authors use a simple math equation as an example of a tame problem. The task at hand (e.g., 2 + 2 = 4) is clear, and only one correct solution exists. The term *wicked* does not indicate the moral nature of a problem but, rather, highlights its complex nature. In contrast to tame problems, wicked problems may be unique; are difficult to define; lack a clear, singular solution or stopping point; and involve a diverse group of stakeholders who may have conflicting priorities.

Experience design problems involve people and are thus inherently wicked because of the complexity of human behavior. Rittel and Webber, along with many others, suggest that wicked problems should be approached differently than tame problems. Wicked problems, like designing experiences, require their own methodology. In this chapter we're going to use design thinking to sequentially organize the content and tools covered thus far into a methodology for tackling wicked experience design problems, which we call "experience design thinking."

Design Thinking

Design thinking has received increasing attention over the last ten-to-twenty years as a broadly applicable and accessible design approach to solve wicked problems. Design thinking provides an ideal process to guide the experience design process. In the following sections we provide background information on design thinking, discuss each stage of the process, and then use this process to provide a sequential structure to the experience design content presented to this point in the book. We'll wrap up the chapter with an official introduction to the process of experience design thinking.

David Kelly, who played founding roles in both the Hasso Plattner Institute of Design at Stanford University, known as the d.school, and the design firm IDEO, was central to synthesizing previous work on the design process to propose a formalized methodology he called "design thinking." Focusing on human values is the foundational mindset for design thinking. Another term often used in conjunction with design thinking is *human-centered design*. The idea is that you can't design anything unless you develop empathy for your targeted participants. The best experience designers are empathetic. They actively seek to understand their participants' perspectives and use them as a guiding influence for the whole design process. They also have a propensity

for forward progress, meaning they move rapidly through the design process without belaboring particular points. For more information on the principles behind design thinking, we encourage you to visit the d.school and IDEO resource websites.[6]

There are several different frameworks for design thinking, but we like the five-stage process used by the d.school:

- Empathize
- Define
- Ideate
- Prototype
- Test[7]

The five stages are often introduced as a linear sequence, but in practice they usually occur as part of a cyclical process. The following subsections provide more details on each stage.

Empathize

In chapter 4 when we were discussing the importance of understanding the people participating in your experience, we promised additional techniques for accomplishing this. Learning to gain empathy for your participants is one of them. *Merriam-Webster* defines *empathy* as "the action of understanding, being aware of, being sensitive to, and vicariously experiencing the feelings, thoughts, and experience of another."[8] To engage in design thinking, you must know who your participants are and invest the necessary time and resources to understand them. It's easy to simply design experience you think would be desirable rather than what your participants really need or want. Taking the time to develop empathy with your participants helps you to view the experience you're designing from their perspective.

Developing empathy when creating experiences for others is especially important because the results of the experiences you design are contingent on the perceptions of your participants. Remember, Clay Shirky told us participants expect their presence to matter in the unfolding action of an experience. In chapter 1 we introduced a figure modified from work by Mat and his colleagues at Brigham Young University that represented the interaction between participants and the elements of an experience; this figure produces perceived results.[9]

In the paper associated with this figure, Mat and his colleagues, drawing on a pool of interdisciplinary literature, identified the following participant elements that influence this interaction:

- Relationships—Any relationship participants have with individuals, both present and not present, that influence their perception of the experience. For example, the participants' social-media connections who express opinions about the experience are one important relationship.
- Thoughts—Any relevant cognitive processing about the experience. What do the participants think about the type of experience you plan to offer?
- Emotions—Feelings that participants bring into the experience and develop during the experience. How do they feel about the experiences you plan to offer?
- Values—Ethical and moral opinions held by participants. Do your participants have pre-existing ethical or moral opinions about the experiences you plan to offer?
- Activities—Physical and mental activities engaged in before or during the experience. This often relates to necessary knowledge and skill that have been acquired during previous experiences that would influence how the participants perceive your experience.
- Memories—Take account of all relevant memories from previous engagements that may influence participants' interpretations of the current experience.
- Personal Characteristics—Pertinent demographic and psychographic characteristics.[10]

Once you identify who your participants will be, you need to make sure you gather as much information related to these elements as possible. To gain empathy with potential participants, consider observing them in their day-to-day contexts. If possible, try to observe them participating in experiences like the one you hope to design. Also, engage with them. Ask them questions to gather information related to their relationships, thoughts, emotions, activities, values, memories, and personal characteristics. This can be accomplished through surveys, in formal interviews, or by observing and talking with participants. Take notes and pictures—anything that helps capture insights and synthesize your findings.

A great example of the benefits of gaining empathy with participants comes from a classic article by Harvard Business School professor Clayton Christensen and his colleagues titled "Finding the Right Job for Your Product."[11] In the article, Christensen recounts how gathering observational data about end users provided their research team with empathetic insights about the job people were "hiring" milkshakes to do for them. When a large fast-food company wanted to improve milkshake sales, they brought in Christensen's team to help them understand the characteristics of the milkshakes that were most important to customers.

One of the team members decided to observe the process of people purchasing and consuming milkshakes. The conclusions drawn from these observations were as follows: most milkshakes were purchased in the morning, they were the only item purchased, purchasers were alone, and they left the store to enjoy their shake. Accordingly, the team realized that shakes were being purchased by commuters who needed something they could consume while driving to work. So much for eggs and bacon! This insight was the direct result of spending the time needed to understand the end users' experiences and the job they were "hiring" milkshakes to do, which was to provide them an on-the-go breakfast.

Good experience designers know that developing empathy with their participants is essential. John Connors, the vice president of event development for Bigsley Event House, believes that the ability to empathize is the most essential trait of great experience designers.[12] Taking time to develop a deep understanding of the people you want to design for will have a dramatic effect on the quality of experiences you create.

Define

Once you've developed a sense of empathy with your participants, it's time to define the most pressing needs you hope to address with the experience. The d.school explains the purpose of the define stage as

> your chance . . . to define the challenge you are taking on, based on what you have learned about your user and about the context. After becoming an instant-expert on the subject and gaining invaluable empathy for the person you are designing for, this stage is about making sense of the widespread information you have gathered.[13]

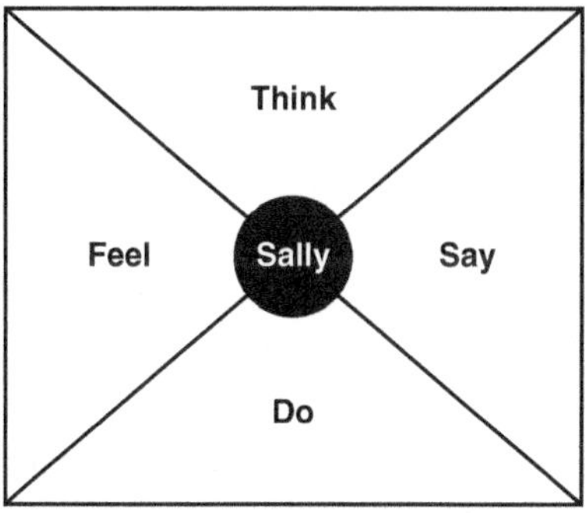

Figure 5.1 Empathy map.

The first step of defining is to organize and synthesize your empathy data. One way to do this is to use an empathy map, a tool originally developed by Dave Gray.[14] To create your own simplified empathy map, draw a circle in the middle of a piece of paper or on a whiteboard. In the middle of the circle write the name of the individual you collected data from. Divide the rest of the circle into four quadrants (see figure 5.1). Label the quadrants "think," "feel," "say," and "do." Now organize your findings by writing the information on sticky notes and placing them in the quadrants where they apply.

When you complete your empathy map, you should have a list of the identified needs and potential insights you gained during the process, which you'll then use to create what the d.school calls a "point of view [POV]"[15] statement. A POV statement is "your reframing of a design challenge into an actionable problem statement."[16] You can use the following rubric to create POV statements:

> "[User] needs to [user's need] because [surprising insight]."[17]

Developing the right POV is critical to the rest of the process. So, you should invest the time necessary to develop a good one. You'll want to look over the empathy data you have gathered to identify the most pressing needs and interesting insights you discovered. At this point, you are engaging in data reduction. You must focus on the most salient one-to-three unique points that must be addressed. If you cannot get focused at this point, you will have too many issues

to respond to and there will not be enough resources to develop the key themes of your experience. It you are still struggling, draft a few different POV statements to see which one resonates most with you and your participants.

This process can get more complicated with some experiences. For example, in developing experiences for children, multiple stakeholders are involved—the child, the parent, or some other adult who will make the decision to purchase or allow the child to participate in the experience. In these cases, you may need to create separate POVs for the children and the adults involved.

Here's a quick example of the POV development process. Let's say you are a hotel manager who wants to design a new check-in procedure for repeat customers. After gathering empathy data, you realize that these customers have several needs that must be met concurrently. They want to feel recognized for their loyalty to your brand, they want to feel at home when they come to your hotel, and they want check-in to be hassle-free and quick. You create the following POV statement based on this information:

> *Our repeat customers want to be personally recognized when checking in because it's nice to feel "at home" when they're on the road, and they want their check-in to be quick and simple.*

You then use this statement along with the empathy map(s) created in the empathize stage to guide the remaining steps of the process. There is no one perfect POV statement. Crafting a POV statement is important, but don't spend too much time wordsmithing. Remember, we told you to be messy; you can go back to modify your POV later if needed.

Ideate

Now that you have both a POV statement and an empathy map (or maps) in hand, you can begin to come up with solutions to address identified needs. Although this is the point where many people start the experience design process, don't make that same mistake! We have found that skipping the empathize and define stages will often result in designing solutions to the wrong problem. Employing experience design thinking requires that you begin ideating only once

you understand your participants and their most compelling needs. Because you've most likely engaged in some type of brainstorming or ideation before, we don't want to spend too much time on this topic, but we would like to offer a word of caution and then highlight a few important best practices.

We add the caution that this sequential process of identifying a problem and then developing solutions works only if you have correctly determined the problem that matters most to your participants. Thomas Wendt has written about this problem-solution paradox: "Problems and solutions evolve together and must be understood together."[18] He also explains that "the linear movement from problem to solution does not leave room for exploring the effects of solutions on the system for which they are designed."[19] So, it is often the case that the designer must move back and forth between the problem and the proposed solutions as each helps further define the other. We believe that these iterations occur in actual design practice but are often not noted in diagrams or descriptions of designing experiences. We empower you to be as nonlinear as needed to design better!

Ideation involves two distinct stages: divergence and convergence. When you engage in divergent ideation, the goal is to come up with as many ideas as quickly as possible. Effective ideation requires you to push perfectionism aside and be open to out-of-the-box and half-baked ideas. For many of us, doing this is difficult. Because we may feel our professional competence is on the line, we usually present only polished solutions. The problem with this approach is that it constrains your ability to come up with novel and innovative ideas. It's common for the first set of ideas during an ideation session to be safe and standard. One way to avoid this pitfall is to force yourself and your design team to generate at least fifty ideas. It can be helpful to write each idea on a sticky note and then place the sticky notes on a table or wall. Remember, during divergent ideating the goal is quantity, not quality. At this point don't worry about feasibility (how much an idea will cost) or viability (whether putting the idea into action is even possible). Let yourself think freely about all potential solutions to the POV statement in question.

When generating ideas, it's also important to make sure your ideating is both fluent and flexible. In the context of ideating, fluency refers to the quantity of ideas produced, flexibility to the variety of ideas produced.[20] Fluent and flexible ideation results in lots of diverse ideas. Check yourself as you ideate to ensure that you're not getting

into a rut of simply coming up with variations of the same theme. Push yourself to be radical and diverse in your solution generation.

Once you've generated a sufficient number of ideas—remember the goal of fifty—you can shift into convergent ideation. The goal here is to sift through the generated ideas to identify those you want to move forward into prototyping. This involves eliminating, combining, and identifying the ideas most promising for solving your stated problem. As you do this, remember to keep the POV statement and your empathy maps in mind because you want to be selecting the ideas you think will resonate with your participants and address their primary needs, not yours or your team's.

The d.school has some great guidance regarding convergence. It is useful to think of the process as convergence or agreement rather than conflict resolution for your design team. It's about working together to select the best solutions for your participants, not defending and promoting favorite ideas. Two ideas we especially like are "Post-it voting" and "the four-category method."[21] With Post-it voting, you allow the ideation group members to vote for their top three or four ideas, and the ideas that receive the most votes move forward into prototyping. With the four-category method, you organize all ideas into four predetermined categories—the d.school suggests these: "the rational choice, the most likely to delight [your participant], the darling [of the group], and the long shot."[22] You then select a few ideas from each category.

Regardless of how you engage in divergent and convergent ideation, remember the goal is to create solutions that address the POV statement in a way that will resonate with participants. You want a solution for them, their needs, and their problems. Ideation should be energizing and fun. You can ideate on your own, but we find that the best ideation sessions are group affairs. The energy of a group ideation session is infectious. Remember, though, you must help the group members understand the importance of rejecting perfectionism and not passing judgment on all the ideas they generate. With these ground rules in place, you should be able to easily come up with some exciting ideas to move into prototyping.

Prototype

Prototyping involves taking the ideas you generated in the previous stage and turning them into physical, actionable artifacts, or what

Eric Ries calls "minimum viable products."[23] While it's easy for most people to think about prototypes for buildings or products, it might be trickier to get your head around prototyping experiences. The d.school's "Introduction to Design Thinking Process Guide" states that "a prototype can be anything that a user can interact with[,] . . . something a user can experience."[24] So what types of experience prototypes could you create to foster interaction? Remember, this could be physical as well as cognitive interaction. Common experience prototypes include low-fidelity mockups of experience settings (e.g., cardboard storefronts), role-play situations (e.g., walking participants through a new hotel check-in experience), storyboards and mock agendas, or experimental versions of a new product that can be tested with participants.

The goal is not to create a final, polished version of your experience but to develop a prototype you can use to facilitate feedback from potential participants. The benefit is that you can find out what works and doesn't work with your experience before investing the time and resources needed to implement the final version. Prototyping is a discovery activity taking place before implementation rather than a production process.

Developing an actionable representation of your experience will also get you to think differently about your ideated solution[s]. When problem-solving, we often default to thinking and talking about solutions. Prototyping forces you to sketch, build, and engage with your ideas in a more tactile fashion. Seymour Papert, a student of the renowned psychologist Jean Piaget, spent his career developing and promoting his theory of constructivism, which suggested that learning happens most effectively when learners build things related to what they are thinking and learning about.[25] Trust us, and Papert, on this one, prototyping will help you gather richer feedback from potential participants and cause you to think more deeply and creatively about your ideas.

We have also used experience maps, a topic we'll cover in depth in chapter 6, as prototypes that allow for vicarious engagement of the experience. Once you know your participants, understand and articulate their needs, and develop a variety of potential solutions to those needs, you are ready to create an experience map. It is a prototyped experience journey. Although you can create a variety of experience prototypes—and we encourage you to be creative about this

process—keep in mind that creating an experience map is an extremely effective prototype approach. It's also important to have the mindset that all experiences are prototypes that can continually be refined.

Test

The testing stage is all about receiving feedback about the prototypes you've created. It's a time to be open to input rather than defensive about your ideas. If you create an experience role-play, walk potential participants through the role-play and then ask for their feedback. If you create a prototype of an experience setting, allow potential participants to interact with the setting and then provide you with feedback. In essence, you're providing testers with a prototyped, interactive experience.

Because gathering feedback is the primary purpose of testing, make sure you prepare to systematically gather as much data as you can. When possible, it's helpful to have multiple testing facilitators who have been assigned specific roles. You can have one person facilitate the testing experience; another person observe the testing process, paying particular attention to testing participants' reactions to the prototype and how they interact with it; and finally, someone to conduct a formal debriefing with participants either individually or in a focus-group setting.

Although testing prototypes with actual participants is ideal, in some situations it's not always feasible. For this reason, we want to show you the versatility of using an experience map, a tool we'll discuss further in chapter 6, as a prototype for testing, with or without participants, using visualization. What we mean by visualization is seeing the prototyped experience in your mind's eye.[26] Using this approach, if you have access to participants, you would use the experience map as a script to help them visualize the experience, perhaps in a focus group. Ask them to close their eyes, and then you describe to them, in as much detail as possible, each touchpoint of the experience. Encourage them to visualize what you're describing and to make notes or to provide feedback either during or after the visualization process.

If you don't have access to participants, you can visualize the experience map yourself. This can be quite effective if you've done your empathy homework, because you will be able to draw on that information

to try to see the experience from your participants' eyes. In fact, visualizing in this way can be extremely useful because you can walk through your experience map from the perspective of different participants who might engage in your experience. Take note of how they might perceive various touchpoints of the experience differently. For example, take any experience and visualize it from the perspective of an adult versus that of a child. Just the difference in height will sometimes point out things that need to be modified. Finally, it can also be beneficial to visualize the experience from a bird's-eye view to see how participants move through the experiencescape you plan or design.

However you decide to test your experience, remember that the goal is to receive and act on feedback. Experience design thinking is an iterative process, meaning that you should take the feedback you received and return to earlier stages of the process to continue revising the design. You may want to go back to tweak your prototypes, or you may find that you need to completely rewrite your POV statement. The more open you are to change and refinement, the better your experience will be in the end.

Summary: Experience Design + Design Thinking

We're excited about the merger of experience design and design thinking into experience design thinking. We believe that the design-thinking approach is an excellent methodology to organize and apply the content and tools covered in the book. It serves as an organizational framework for experience design. It lays out a process, which when applied will produce innovative experience design solutions. The next two chapters will introduce you to experience mapping, a topic alluded to earlier in this chapter. Learning how to map macroexperiences and then design their constituent microexperiences will allow you to create extremely useful experience prototypes. If you take the time to use all the tools you will be exposed to in the remaining chapters in the book and then use the methodology of experience design thinking to apply them, we know that you will create effective, innovative, and high-quality experiences.

CHAPTER SIX

Designing the Experience Journey

IN CHAPTER 4 we took a granular perspective of experiences to examine the essential elements of experiencescapes. In this chapter, we're going to change our perspective and assume an aerial view to observe how each microexperience links together to build the journey that is our macroexperience. To do this, we're going to talk about public bathrooms, Disneyland, and mapmaking. But to start things off, let's look first at the relationship between designing experiences and composing music to learn two key experience design principles.

Perfect Pitch

Mat enjoys listening to classical music while he writes. He especially loves Johann Sebastian Bach's cello suites. Great composers, like Bach, understand how to combine notes, chords, tempo, instruments, voices, and other musical elements to create a holistic musical experience. True classics, like Bach's cello suites, continue to captivate listeners today. There are few experiences that can lay claim to a similar shelf life.

Music composition provides an excellent analogy to convey two important experience design insights that will play a key role in the topics we're discussing in this chapter: intentionality and heterogeneity.

Intentionality

Consider the degree of intentionality that goes into composing a symphony. Each note, among hundreds if not thousands, is meticulously placed to complement those around it and fit into the flow of the entire piece. The whole musical score requires intentional arrangement. It's absurd even to consider a composer masterfully crafting certain sections of a piece while simply throwing random notes together without rhyme or reason in other sections. Even someone with an untrained musical ear would easily be able to determine sections that were intentionally arranged and those that were not. And, most likely, the dissonance of the unintentional sections would mask the harmony of the intentional ones.

Designing experiences is similar; all notes (i.e., microexperiences) require intentional design. You've probably had experiences in which meticulous attention to detail was paid to certain elements of an experience, whereas other aspects obviously received no forethought. Consider the public bathroom. You may have had an otherwise great restaurant, movie, music, shopping, or amusement park experience marred by a visit to a dirty public bathroom in the venue. No matter how great the rest of the experience has been, this one negative microexperience can derail an otherwise positive macroexperience. After encountering a dirty bathroom, you may even start thinking, "If the bathrooms are overlooked, what else about this experience has been ignored?" As a designer, you should make sure that all microexperiences receive the same degree of intentionality to provide uniform quality across your designed experiences. This means, among other things, that your bathrooms need to be clean.

In some cases, intentional attention to prosaic microexperiences, like using the facilities, can be leveraged into a competitive distinction. Buc-ee's Travel Centers are a good case in point. If you live in Texas, you already know what we're talking about; but if you're a non-Texan, let us explain. Buc-ee's is a gas station chain in Texas known for, among other things, perennially winning the "America's Best Restroom" contest. In an article in *Texas Monthly* magazine titled "Holy Crap,"

author Jason Cohen describes the attention to detail Buc-ee's gives to the restroom experience. So sure that their bathroom experience is amazing, Buc-ee's actively promotes it with billboards showing messages like "The Top Two Reasons to Stop at Buc-ee's: Number 1 and Number 2" and "Restrooms You Have to Pee to Believe."[1]

Walt Disney, experience designer extraordinaire, innately understood the importance of intentionally designing all microexperiences. Walt's focus on all details of an experience fostered the Disney theme parks' mantra of "everything speaks."[2] This means that every element within an experience sends a message to participants in the same way that each note in a symphony sends a message to listeners. A clean bathroom says, "This is a clean place because we care about the details of your experience," whereas a dirty bathroom says, "We're overwhelmed with running other things and we didn't have time to get this cleaned." You want to make sure that all elements share a cohesive message because even one discordant element can ruin the harmony of the experience.

This principle of "everything speaks" applies to all elements of every microexperience within a macroexperience. Walt Disney's attention to detail in the design of Disneyland is legendary. One example is his insistence that each area of Disneyland have unique and theme-appropriate pavement because "you can get information about a changing environment through the soles of your feet."[3] Disney knew that even the pavement at Disneyland would send a message, albeit a potentially subconscious one, and he wanted that message to align with and contribute to the rest of the experience elements in the park. Achieving this degree of comprehensive intentionality takes sustained effort, but it often marks the difference between forgettable and unforgettable experiences.

Heterogeneity

Merriam-Webster defines *heterogeneity* as "the quality or state of consisting of dissimilar or diverse elements." We know this word is a mouthful, but it's more descriptive of what we're trying to convey than are terms like *variety* or *uniqueness*. It speaks to arrangements of diverse elements in unique but intentional, rather than random, ways. It has connections to words like *creativity* and *innovation* because they all deal with bringing diverse elements together in new ways. We also

think that because it's probably not a word you use every day, its novelty will help it stick in your head.

Okay, so now you know what heterogeneity means, but what does it have to do with music and experiences? Bob loves to sing. He has performed in choirs and barbershop quartets, and recently he had the distinct honor of performing with his church choir in Carnegie Hall in New York City. He can tell you that great music does not usually consist simply of the ad nauseam repetition of a small handful of the same notes. Most compositions begin with a melody and then build on variations of the melody to create a complete piece.

Great experience designers employ the principle of heterogeneity by implementing a variety of microexperiences drawn from across the experience-type framework to create diversity in macroexperiences. The sequence and type of microexperiences are intentionally arranged to positively engage participants throughout the course of the macroexperience. Heterogeneity keeps us engaged as listeners and participants. The best musicians and experience designers know how to use rises and falls in action, dissonance and harmony, and ritual and novelty, among other techniques, to create multifaceted experiences for their end users. Homogenous experiences, on the other hand, are made up of a finite number of elements arranged in repetitive patterns. Homogenous experiences lull participants into system 1 thinking. Heterogeneous experiences keep your participants engaged because they actively enjoy the moment while anticipating what's going to happen next.

You're probably thinking, "Okay, so how do I actually go about infusing those principles into my experiences?" Good question—so let's explore some specific experience design approaches to do just that.

Experience Mapping

Over the last decade the concept of experience mapping has become a hot topic as a core experience design approach. The awareness that experiences matter has led people to realize that they need a way to conceptually orchestrate what the experiences they provide look like for end users. Although different types of experience maps exist (e.g., service blueprints, customer journey maps, experience maps, existing and future state maps),[4] all share a similar focus on mapping the microexperiences that make up macroexperiences. In this chapter

we're going to teach you how to use experience maps to create experience prototypes. Experience mapping can also be used to evaluate and re-envision existing experiences. It is an essential and versatile tool for all experience designers.

Key Elements of Experience Maps

Experience maps come in many different shapes and sizes. Our goal is to introduce you to what we believe are the key components of any experience map. This will give you a starting point to begin building your own experience maps. If you want to learn more about this topic, there are some great resources out there that will allow you to expand your experience-mapping toolkit. Here is a list of a few of these resources:

- *Mapping Experiences* by Jim Kalbach
- Oracle's website, Designingcx.com
- The experience-mapping resources at Adaptivepath.org

To be a proficient experience designer, you need to be comfortable with the following experience-mapping elements: personas, intentionality, touchpoints, reactions, and front- and backstage contributors.

Personas

Before you build an experience map, you need to decide whose journey you're mapping. We're not talking about a simple target audience or market segment; we're talking about the specific individuals you envision as being potential participants of the experience you're designing. You might ask why. Well, first, we've already explained that experiences are individually perceived. Second, good experience design needs to always be participant focused. You're not designing *your* ideal experience; you're designing the ideal experience for a specific participant. When you use experience mapping to evaluate an existing experience, you can work with real participants to build a map that reflects their actual experience. When using experience maps to design new experiences, you don't have actual participants yet, but you can still create participant-focused experience maps using *personas.*

Personas are simply a graphic representation of a participant or a synthesized representation of multiple participants. To build a persona, you first need to think about the potential participants of the experience you're designing. Traditional marketing approaches used to focus on target markets built on composite group characteristics. But often, the resulting "average" person did not represent an actual individual. Building personas is an attempt to be more grounded; you need to get to know actual individuals who represent your participant groups. This knowledge could come from your personal experience with representative participants, but it's even better when you can go out to talk with and observe individuals who fit your participant profile. Jim Kalbach, author of *Mapping Experience*, suggests gathering the following types of information to create a persona:

- **Demographics**—This category includes age, gender, ethnicity, and any other relevant demographic indicators.
- **Psychographics**—Whereas demographics usually deals with observable characteristics, psychographics includes less observable individual traits like attitudes, beliefs, and aspirations.
- **Relevant behaviors**—These are the behaviors or actions (e.g., habits, hobbies, professional activities) with relevance to the experience you will be designing.
- **Needs and Pain Points**—What are needs you can meet and pains you can relieve with the experience you're designing?[5]

As mentioned, you can gather this information directly from actual people, or you can pull from your design team's experience to create what Kalbach calls a "proto-persona."[6] Although it's always preferable to create personas based on real individuals, proto-personas can serve as a nice workaround if time and resources are short. In some cases—when developing a new product, for example—there may be individuals who have never seen or used the product, so the only potential participant available is the one you vicariously construct. Either way, you want to create personas for each distinct participant group you foresee engaging in your experience.

Personas are usually no more than page-length descriptions and are often laid out as a graph. They need to include a name, picture, and short description of the person (you can use pseudonyms for the purpose of confidentiality, but personas built with information from real

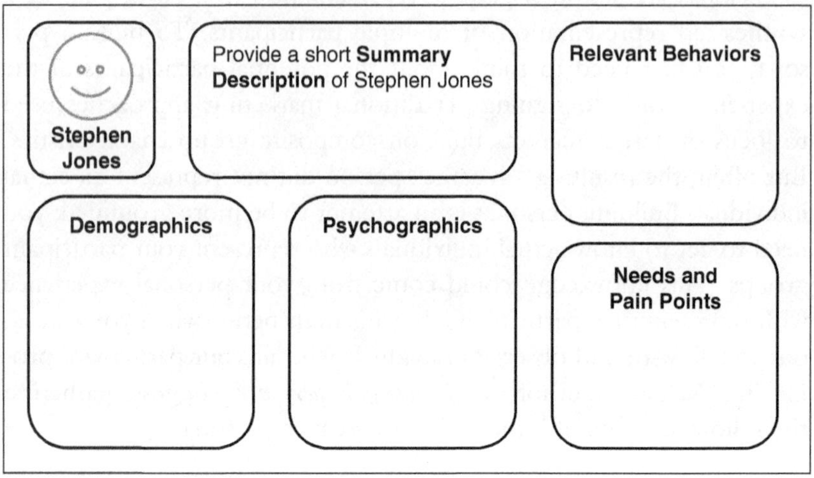

Figure 6.1 The persona template.

end users will be the most helpful), along with information from the four aforementioned areas: demographics, psychographics, relevant behaviors, and needs and pain points. You will want to display your personas prominently so that you and your team can refer to them throughout the design process. It's common to place a smaller version of a persona directly on a journey map to keep the process explicitly end-user focused. Figure 6.1 is a template you can use to create your own personas, though there really are no specific rules you must follow; the goal is to create a graphic artifact that will help you keep the participant in your mind's eye as you proceed through the design process.

One note of caution is necessary when it comes to the use of personas. Avoid the pitfall of using personas as the filter through which all participants are evaluated. Personas can serve as a helpful design tool to keep you focused on designing for others but are never a replacement for continuous efforts to empathize with your participants. Yes, you can reconstruct your personas as you learn more about the participants.

Intentionality in Mapping Experiences

Now that you have a few specific personas in mind, you need to think about what you want these individuals to get out of the experience you're designing. Or better yet, ask the people behind your personas

what they want to get out of the experience in question. What results will you need to target for them within each microexperience so that together these experiences will culminate in a specific macroexperience outcome? Thinking carefully about results will help you increase the likelihood that the experience you design will deliver results you and your participants value. As you begin to create an experience map, you need to focus on a few primary macroexperience results. These serve as the end destination for the experience you're creating. Once you know where you want to help your personified participants to go, you're ready to start thinking about how to take them there.

When you are thinking about intentional outcomes, focus on only a few key effects you want the macroexperience to facilitate for participants. There is a tendency to try to expand the desired outcomes list to encompass all possible positive results. We recommend that you keep your list of targeted outcomes short and focused. If you select too many outcomes, not only are you likely to lack the resources to achieve them all, but you are also likely to lack the ability to give each outcome adequate attention.

Touchpoints

At this point you have identified a specific group of participants and a desired outcome you want your experience to produce. Now it's time to think about the microexperiences you'll need to design and how to sequence them to create the macroexperience that will lead your participants on a journey resulting in the outcome. In mapping vernacular, we refer to microexperiences as touchpoints. A touchpoint represents a specific time and place during an experience in which a participant interacts with designed experience elements. Some touchpoints will be short and others long. Regardless, they represent the time a participant is actively interacting with the experiencescape elements you have intentionally orchestrated. The combined, sequential touchpoints represent the journey your participant will take; they make up the graphically displayed experience map.

Although there is no fixed rule regarding how many touchpoints an experience map should include, you should especially try to account for all touchpoints that will provide opportunities for participants to be actively engaged, thereby shaping their perceived outcomes and resulting memories. You don't need to account for all the time in an

experience journey. In fact, you probably can't anyway. The touchpoints you identify and design represent the interactions that must be present for participants to have the opportunity to co-create the experience you've envisioned.

We should note that it's common for individuals to serendipitously add touchpoints of their own making along an experience journey. This is fine, to be expected, and often why accounts differ across individuals participating in the same experience. Your design should result in personal narratives of the experience with some commonality, but it's okay if there are some individual nuances as well. These are the collateral outcomes of the experience, and experiences that are well designed are more likely to produce positive rather than negative outcomes.

We like to use sticky notes when building experience maps because they allow for quick and easy building and revising. You can also use online collaborative whiteboard platforms like Mural.co, Realtimeboard.com, or Lucidchart.com. When you first start identifying touchpoints, don't worry too much about sequence. Simply start writing down potential touchpoints, one per sticky note, and place the notes on your working surface. If you're working as a team, posting the sticky notes on a wall is a great way to get everyone up and moving.

After your initial effort to generate touchpoints, you can start arranging the touchpoints sequentially. Using sticky notes facilitates modifications and additions to your map as it's developed. As you will discover, sequence matters, and rearranging touchpoint order can help you discover new design insights. For example, why not serve the salad after rather than before the entree? The French do this often so that the vinegars in the salad do not interfere with the palate's ability to taste wine. But doing this would be a novel change in the typical American dining sequence. As you're arranging your touchpoints, remember to consider principles we've discussed earlier in the book like the peak-end rule.[7] Make sure you're intentionally building peaks and making final touchpoints meaningful.

Some experiences are not linear and thus give participants freedom to create and sequence their touchpoints in unique ways. Consider a community festival. In such an experience, touchpoints do not happen in the same order for all participants because the festival patrons are free to wander. In these cases, where a set linear configuration doesn't exist, you need to give some thought to which touchpoints are essential for the success of the overall experience and devise ways to attract patrons to them. One example would be to highlight the main attractions on

a printed diagram layout given to patrons. Or you could give away a book of passes or tickets to the main attractions to ensure participation in these defining touchpoints of the experience. These are among the many things to consider as you create your experience maps.

While we recognize that not all experience journeys are linear and that they may involve branching paths, we recommend that you keep things simple for your first few maps. Build some straightforward maps first and then get more ambitious. Also, remember that a full experience map covers all three experience phases—anticipation, participation, and reflection—from the moment an individual learns about the experience until after the experience has ended and he or she begins to tell other people about it.[8]

Reactions

The next question to consider is, How do you want people to respond to each touchpoint? Reactions are the primary response an end user will have to a touchpoint. When identifying touchpoint reactions, remember that they should align with and contribute to the overall macroexperience results that are intended. The best experience designers are masters at orchestrating touchpoints to promote a cohesive, intentional macroexperience feel.

Mat is good friends with one such master experience designer, John Connors, the former vice president of event development for Bigsley Event House. Bigsley stages The Color Run™ (TCR), which consists of untimed 5K races in which participants have colored powder thrown on them. Bigsley leveraged this simple concept into the largest running series in the world with over five million racers in more than thirty-five countries participating since their founding in 2012. Needless to say, the company's event development team knows how to design unique and engaging experiences.

To continually improve the TCR experience, John created what he calls The Color Run Event Model (see figure 6.2). This simple yet powerful framework, which draws inspiration from Disney's mantra "everything speaks," is built on four key questions:

1. What do customers *want*?
2. What do you as the experience designer *want* customers to say?
3. What is your experience *actually* saying?
4. What are customers *actually* saying?[9]

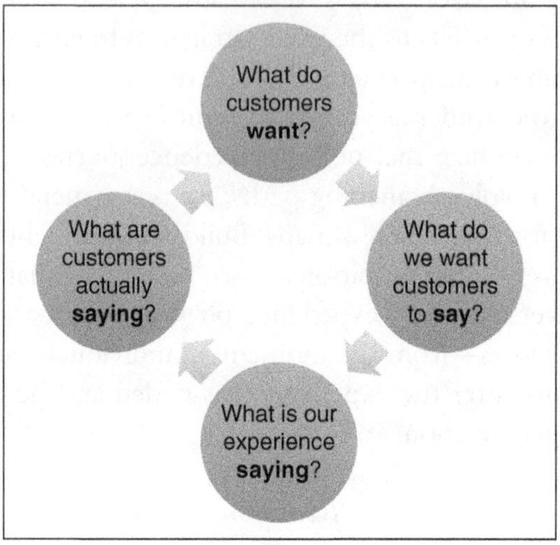

Figure 6.2 The Color Run Event Model.

As you design an experience, have some idea of the end user's needs that you're attempting to meet. You must then deduce what you hope people will say about the experience you're providing—their reactions to it. Next, critically examine each touchpoint and its relevant experiencescape elements to determine whether these touchpoints are "saying" the same things that you want your participants to say. For example, if you want your customers to say, "This is a friendly company," you want to make sure you're intentionally doing things to make touchpoints friendly. This might include ensuring that all employees who will have face-to-face contact with customers are trained to smile when introducing themselves. Once you've worked to ensure alignment between your desired reactions and designed touchpoints, you need to listen to what customers are actually saying about your experience through formal customer feedback channels or on social media. If they're saying what you hoped they would say, you know you're on the right track; if not, you need to make some changes.

John wants TCR participants to say, "This is the happiest 5K on the planet" and "This is a well-run event."[10] These two statements, or reactions, guide the design and evaluation of all TCR events: Do the online registration process, the onsite racer-bib pickup, the starting chute experience, and the color stations all lead people to say, "This is

the happiest 5K on the planet"? If not, TCR makes modification so that customers are saying what the company wants them to say. A side benefit of identifying a small number of key reactions is that doing this will simplify your training process. The overarching directive behind John's training of staff, volunteers, and employees is to do whatever it takes, within reason, to help people say, "This is the happiest 5K on the planet" and "This is a well-run event."

Consider another Disney example. In designing Disneyland, Walt set out to create the happiest place on earth. One of the things he wanted people to say about Disneyland was that it is a clean place, in contrast to the typical amusement park at that time. To ensure that this would be something people would say, Walt made sure that patrons were never farther than thirty steps from a trash can. He calculated this number by figuring out through observation the average number of steps people would take while holding trash before tossing it aside.[11] It may seem like an insignificant design decision, but it shows the importance of knowing what you want people to say about your experience and then making sure you're designing it, all the way down to the number of available trash cans, to facilitate that reaction. It takes real discipline to keep focused on matching touchpoints with intended macroexperience results, but doing so will enhance the overall quality of the experiences you design.

To thoroughly implement this process, you need to explicitly state the types of reactions you want people to have during each touchpoint along your experience map. These represent the keywords essential to intentionally designing your experience as well as to interfacing through the web with customers who are searching for the type of experiences you are providing. These keywords are the conduit through which niche customers will find you. These words represent what they are looking for.

The customer experience team at Oracle suggests that you write these reactions as specific statements or thoughts your end user will have at each touchpoint.[12] For example, "That was the easiest check-in experience I've ever had" or "The customer service here is incredible." Write these reactions on separate sticky notes and place them directly above their associated touchpoint. It is helpful to use the same color sticky notes for all touchpoints and a different color for reactions.

With touchpoints identified and organized along a journey that (1) has been designed for specific personas and (2) has associated

reactions paired with each touchpoint, you have a complete experience map. A map with linear touchpoints and end-user reactions represents the most basic of experience maps. Next we're going to ask you to think about the resources needed to implement each touchpoint.

Front- and Backstage Contributors

Oracle has created a customer experience outreach division that conducts free experience-mapping workshops around the world and hosts a website, Designingcx.com, with some great experience-mapping resources. Oracle encourages experience designers to think about the front-stage (i.e., onstage) and backstage contributors associated with each touchpoint.[13] They use theater terminology, which has been employed by other experience design thinkers like B. Joseph Pine II and James H. Gilmore,[14] to indicate the people and things end users will interact with during a touchpoint (frontstage) and the people and things they won't interact with that are necessary to facilitate the touchpoint (backstage). If we think of a restaurant experience, frontstage contributors would include servers, décor, seating arrangements, menus, and food. Backstage contributors would include the chef and other kitchen staff, systems used to manage seating assignments, dishwashing, and the supply chain behind the food prepared in the kitchen.

You could really dive deep into each of these areas, especially the backstage contributors, but the key is to focus on the most relevant contributors for each touchpoint. These are the ones you will need to control or manage to successfully implement the touchpoint. The other nice thing about identifying these contributors is that doing so forces you to think holistically about all the working parts necessary to bring your experience to life. Because—let's say it one last time together—"everything speaks."

To add front- and backstage contributors to your map, use differently colored sticky notes for each and place each note below its respective touchpoint. It's also worth noting that some touchpoints won't have both front- and backstage contributors. That's okay; do your best to flesh out your journey map as much as possible. Don't worry about including every possible contributor you can think of; instead, focus on those that are most salient to the experience and that you have some degree of control over.

Completing the Experience Map

A comprehensive experience map will include touchpoints that span the anticipation, participation, and reflection phases of the experience, along with participant reactions and front- and backstage contributors. As you create an experience map, remember to keep the guiding personas in mind so that the experience is designed to meet the personas' identified needs and desires. It is helpful, remember, to use differently colored sticky notes for each experience-mapping element. This will help you quickly navigate and organize your experience map.

Figure 6.3 provides an example of a simple experience map for a concert. A real experience map would, of course, include additional touchpoints, but this one does include all three phases and provides a visual example of what an experience map would look like. You'll notice the reactions are quotes from participants. Notice also that we've identified relevant front- and backstage contributors.

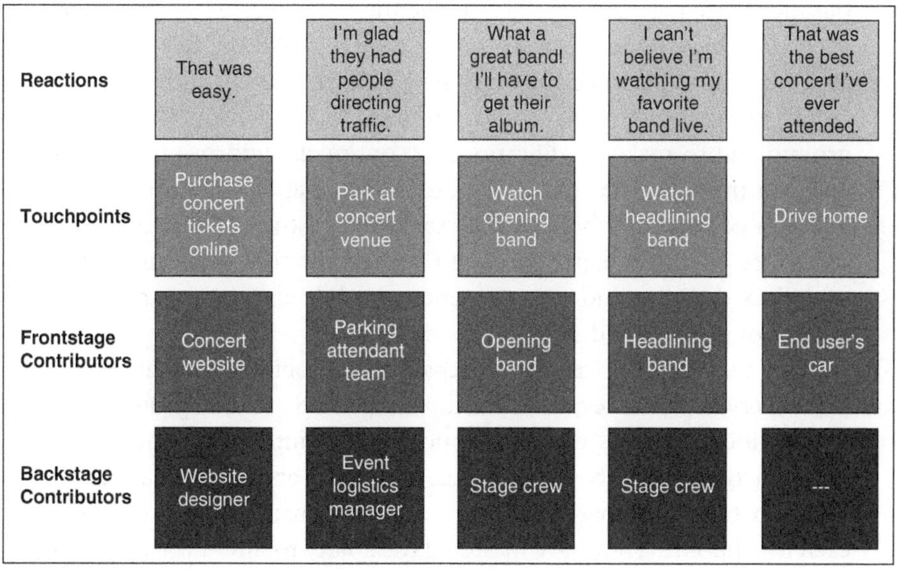

Figure 6.3 Example experience map inspired by Oracle's experience-mapping resources.

Summary: Structuring Experiences

In chapter 4 we looked at the smallest building blocks of microexperiences, the experiencescape elements. In this chapter, we zoomed out to look at the macroexperience structure. Although these dramatic shifts in perspective may seem a bit dizzying, as an experience designer you must be able to think simultaneously about the minutiae and the big picture to ensure that all pieces are working harmoniously. Experience maps are a great way to create a prototype of the experience you're designing. It builds structure and helps pull together key elements into a graphic representation of the experience. As a prototype, it's also meant to be modified. This is not a finished product but, rather, the first draft of a working plan for what your experience might look like. At this point it's not something you need to defend to relevant stakeholders; instead, it's a tool to solicit feedback from them to make the design better.

Experience maps will go through multiple iterations as you work through the experience design process. Your experience maps should also continue to evolve as you start to provide the experiences they outline. Once participants start interacting with your designed experiences, you have gone live and are operating in real time. Keep working at seeing the experience through their eyes. These insights will allow you to tweak your experience maps to reflect what is happening on the ground and to make modifications to continually improve the experience. In this way, the role of the experience map will transition from a design of what will be to a representation of the experience as currently provided. An experience map is a flexible tool that can be used to design, describe, and refine experiences while also serving as a visual artifact of previously delivered experiences.

Now that we've covered the steps for developing an aerial view of the experience journey, it's time to zoom back to the ground-level view to focus on individual experience touchpoints and the transitions between them. The best experience designers are able to seamlessly switch between the big picture of experience maps and the details of each touchpoint. They have mastered the ability to intentionally design each microexperience so that each contributes to a cohesive macroexperience. In the next chapter we'll walk you through the process of using the touchpoint template to design intentional microexperiences.

CHAPTER SEVEN

Touchpoints and Transitions

IN THE ART Institute of Chicago you will find Georges Seurat's masterpiece *A Sunday on La Grande Jatte*, painted in 1884 (see figure 7.1). Seurat was a postimpressionist painter who helped develop a technique called pointillism, which involved using small dots of paint as opposed to more traditional brushstrokes. When viewed up close, pointillist paintings appear to be a random collection of colored dots, but when you step back, the dots merge to form a coherent, vibrant image. To create works of art using this technique, the artist must intentionally place and color each dot to make sure they all work in harmony to create the desired image.

An experience journey is like a pointillist painting: it is formed by combining a series of touchpoints designed to elicit specific reactions and to ultimately achieve the intended results of the macroexperience. To build an experience out of touchpoints, you should give each one, in terms of content and placement, the same attention as a master artist gives to his or her work. It takes time to create quality experiences, just as it takes time to create great works of art (it took Seurat two years to paint *A Sunday on La Grande Jatte*), but your efforts and

Figure 7.1 A Sunday on La Grande Jatte (1884–1886) by Georges Seurat. Courtesy of the Art Institute of Chicago / Art Resource, New York.

attention to detail will be rewarded. Luckily, we have a tool that we think will prove helpful in the design of intentional touchpoints.

The Touchpoint Template

Think of experience maps as a bird's-eye view of the full experience journey you're designing from beginning to end. They include all the touchpoints needed to produce the desired results of the experience. Once you have identified and sequenced your touchpoints, including end-user reactions and front- and backstage contributors, you're ready to start working through the design of each.

To help you accomplish this, we have developed what we call "the touchpoint template." This is a one-page model of each experience touchpoint, and it will help you pull together and apply the topics we've covered thus far in the book. The template also introduces a few additional topics—co-creation, which we will discuss at more length in this chapter, and technical and artistic factors, which will be covered in chapter 9. In one of his previously published books,

Bob and his coauthor, Barbara Schlatter, have called a similar technique "framing" and have recommended its use for designing leisure experiences.[1] The version we recommend here expands on this earlier work and incorporates new content and techniques. Remember, the touchpoint design process, like almost all aspects of experience design, is iterative, so we recommend that you use a pencil to complete early versions of the template.

Modeling a Microexperience

Each touchpoint template is a model of a microexperience that will contribute to the intended results of the macroexperience. Each template specifies the interactions that participants will have with the designed experiencescape elements. As such, the templates also identify the elements the experience designer will need to have in place to enable the microexperience to occur. We'll walk you through a case example shortly, but first consider the main features of the touchpoint template (see figure 7.2):

- Sequence Number (where the touchpoint fits within the experience; may change as you further refine the experience)
- Touchpoint Title
- Experience Type (the type of experience the touchpoint represents, e.g., prosaic to transformational)
- Desired Reaction
- Desired Results
- Experiencescape Elements
- Designed Interactions
- Contributors
- Desired Co-creation Level
- Enhancements (more to come on these in chapter 9)
- Transition

As you may have noticed, much of the information you need to complete the template can be pulled directly from your completed experience map, including the touchpoint name, the desired reaction(s), and the front- and backstage contributors. We've already covered most of the content you need to know to complete the template aside from co-creation and technical and artistic factors. We're going to discuss co-creation shortly, but we'll save a more in-depth conversation of

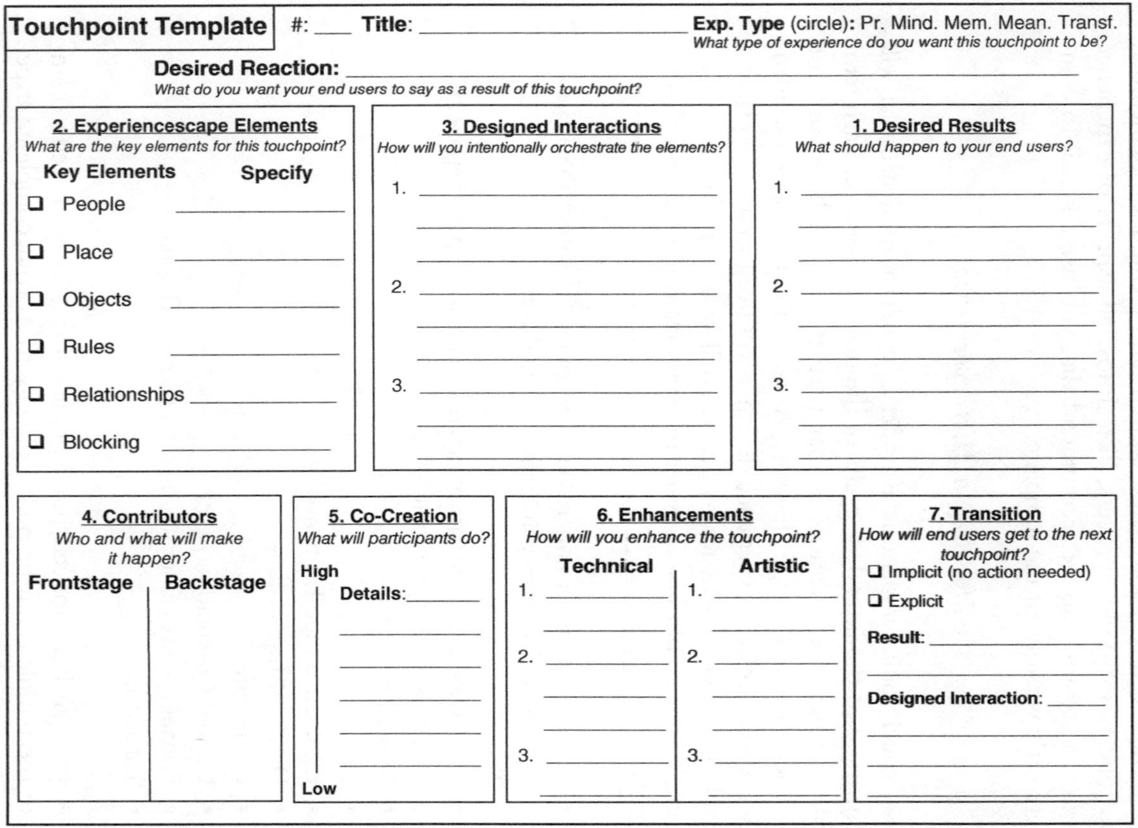

Figure 7.2 Touchpoint template.

experience enhancements for chapter 9. We'll first walk you through each section of the template and then provide a few examples of the template in action.

We recommend that you complete the template in the same order in which we introduced its components. To guide you through the process, we have numbered each section in the template to indicate the correct order of completion. When designing experiences, we start by thinking about desired results, and that's why this box is first even though in terms of implementation sequence desired results are last. This is often called backward design and implements Steven Covey's famous admonition to "begin with the end in mind."[2] We have also included the question you need to address in each section as an italicized subtitle. Before delving into the separate sections, make sure to fill out the top portion of the template, including the touchpoint number, title, and experience type, along with the desired end-user reaction you articulated during the experience-mapping process. It's easier to get somewhere if you know where you are going.

Think of the desired reaction as a rough draft of your desired results. You'll want to create results that logically stem from the reaction. You should have one-to-three desired results for each touchpoint. As you consider possible results, think about the recommended research-based experience results discussed back in chapter 2. As a refresher, here are a few of them:

- Facilitate positive emotions
- Engage attention
- Develop and strengthen relationships
- Promote competence
- Foster freedom to choose

The foregoing list is a great starting point for thinking about potential desired results. At this point, these generic results can be refined to directly apply to the experience being designed. When staging a weekend ski clinic, for example, "promote competence" can be transformed into "participants will improve their ability to complete plow turns." Also, remember to keep in mind the importance of matching experience types and desired results. You can't produce transformational results with a prosaic touchpoint.

After determining your desired results, in some instances you may need to divert from the process order we have specified. Whether the designer should identify elements of the experiencescape to be used before the interactions necessary to execute the results desired will vary depending on the experience being designed. For example, your design problem may be to develop an experience using a specific venue the client already owns and wants to utilize. In this case, the recommended process order works fine. Consider, however, the need to create experiences for a cohort of employees with the desired results of improving esprit de corps and teamwork. In this case, the interactions necessary to accomplish this would likely receive priority attention and the experiencescape elements necessary to support the interactions would be identified after the interactions are designed. In all cases, you want to carefully consider which experiencescape elements are going to be most essential; it is frequently the case that one or two of them will receive priority attention in a given template. Identify each essential element by type and provide a short description.

When designing the interactions you want to facilitate, be expansive in the possibilities you consider. For example, there are many interactions that can be included, among them interactions between your participants and staff, between participants and experiencescape elements, and between participants. You should have at least one designed interaction for each desired result. This way you ensure that there is an intentional causal path to each result desired.

Remember, it's not always the case that experiencescape elements are identified before interactions with them are designed. It is most likely the case that in the design process you will iterate back and forth between these two essential design details. As demonstrated, in some cases you will focus on designing interactions first, and in others you will initially review available or required experiencescape elements and then design the interactions.

The fourth section, contributors, asks, "Who and what will make [the designed interaction] happen?" You will have started answering this question during experience mapping, so revisit your map to address this question. Note both the front- and backstage contributors who will be involved in delivering this touchpoint. The remaining three sections need a bit more introduction. We're going to devote space in this chapter to introducing co-creation and transitions, but you'll have to wait until chapter 9 for a full treatment of enhancements.

Co-creation

Moviemakers and other media planners use a technique they call "storyboarding" to plan the sequential order of scenes in a movie as well as to sketch out and note the critical interactional details of each scene (i.e., blocking the action). The process of experience mapping is like this process. Both storyboarding and experience mapping serve the role of sequencing and outlining key stages of the story or experience. One difference between traditional storyboarding and experience mapping is the role of end users, your participants. When a screenwriter or a director creates a storyboard, he or she knows that the actors will adhere to their scripted roles, with perhaps some small degree of ad-libbing. Experience designers, in contrast, need to recognize that their end users are participants who will often want to play a more active, co-creative role when they engage in the designed experience. Remember, Clay Shirky told us that participants are different than end users; they want to affect outcome. This desire needs to be anticipated and accounted for in the design.

In previous chapters we discussed the interactive, co-creative nature of experiences. *Business Dictionary* defines *co-creation* as "a business strategy focusing on customer experience and interactive relationships. Co-creation allows and encourages a more active involvement from the customer to create a value rich experience."[3] Since its inception the concept of co-creation has been a companion piece to discussions about the experience economy. C. K. Prahalad and Venkat Ramaswamy suggest that before the experience economy, "customers were [seen as] 'outside the firm,'" but "consumers now seek to exercise their influence in every part of the business system. . . . Consumers want to interact with firms and thereby 'co-create' value."[4] Prahalad and Ramaswamy propose that companies "need to create . . . experience environment[s] within which . . . [end users] can create their own unique personalized experience."[5]

Be sure to read in chapter 10 the examples of how corporations are developing keywords and strategies for implementing experiences. Often experiences and their provision have become elements of corporate strategic planning and are included as corporate goals and action plans.

Shirky uses a bar as an example of an experience environment in which customers co-create value through their participation: "The bar

owner is in the same curious business of offering value above the products and services he sells, value that is created by the customers for one another."[6] Think of how the interactions between bar patrons Norm Peterson and Cliff Clavin co-created value in the classic TV series *Cheers.*[7] We are certain your favorite bar has the same characteristics that made Cheers a favorite.

Modern consumers don't want to be handed cookie-cutter products, services, and experiences; they want to help co-create the products, services, and experiences. This is especially true of millennials. They want participatory experiences. Bob has just returned from Buenos Aires, where he and his wife took a cooking class where they learned how to make *empanadas.* Also attending the class were a couple and two millennials who were traveling around the world. Mrs. Norma Soued,[8] who conducts the small-group classes in her lovely condominium in the Palermo neighborhood, told Bob that many of her participants are single young people traveling around the world looking for unusual things they can do. Airbnb addressed this desire for authentic and unique travel experiences by introducing an "Experiences" category in 2017, allowing people to book experiences like flying in a prop plane or learning how to swallow fire, all provided by locals.[9]

If you recall our discussion of experience phases, you will remember that each experience has an anticipation, participation, and reflection phase. We find it helpful to think about co-creation a bit differently within each phase. Drawing from work done by Mat and his colleague Andrew Lacanienta, we reframe co-creation as *co-design* during the anticipation phase, *co-actualization* during the participation phase, and *co-curation* during the reflection phase.[10] In other words, think about ways you can invite your end users to participate in designing (anticipation phase), actualizing (participation phase), and curating (reflection phase) their experiences.

As wonderful as co-creation is, you'll want to manage it. Some touchpoints may have a lot of co-creation and others not so much. Altering the amount from touchpoint to touchpoint will shift demands on participants' energy and attention as the experience moves through time and will create variety and interest in your macroexperience. Let's look briefly at a few examples.

Co-design is probably the most widely applied strategy because it involves any effort to involve participants during the anticipation

phase. Many companies have strong customer feedback loop mechanisms, often called voice-of-the-customer systems, to help gather customer insights and have these insights influence product, service, or experience development. At the individual level, opportunities for customers to customize a product or experience before purchase/participation facilitate co-designing opportunities. When booking a cruise, for example, would-be travelers consider the options available, such as cabin types, dining plan options, and shore excursion selections.

Co-actualization occurs once end users begin to interact with the designed product, service, or experience and can influence outcomes. Think carefully about which touchpoints in the participation phase warrant higher levels of co-actualization. Mat's father, Verle, made some intentional co-actualization decisions when designing the type of white-water–rafting experience he wanted his customers to have. Whereas some outfitters offer full-service trips where passengers' tents and cots are set up for them each night, Verle decided that giving all the participants the chance to select and set up their own campsites would build more group camaraderie. He also decided that guides would handle all food preparation so that guests could enjoy and explore each campsite. Verle felt he could provide the best experience with high co-actualization during camp setup and low co-actualization for meal preparation. There's no one right way to foster co-creation; the key is using opportunities for co-creation to help the experience produce desired outcomes for your participants.

Co-curation is probably the most overlooked opportunity for co-creation. We often put so much effort into designing and providing experiences that when they conclude, we have no energy or plan to intentionally engage with our participants during the reflection phase. Thinking about co-curation strategies can help you avoid this oversight. Co-curation can be as simple as sending a follow-up thank-you note or a short customer feedback survey. More proactive examples of co-curation could involve strategies to assist participants in the curation of their memories of the experience. The National Parks Service does this with its park passport and its Junior Ranger program that encourages patrons to collect stamps, stickers, pins, and ranger badges at each park they visit. The National Parks Service also sells various books and vests patrons can use to display their memorabilia, and the books' blank pages remind them of the parks they still need to visit.

Affordance

Another topic closely related to co-creation is affordance—the number of different types of interactions a product or experience offers. A ball, water, and a sandbox are high-affordance play objects that provide numerous unstructured play opportunities for children. Contrast these with a low-affordance play object like a windup toy monkey that plays a drum. Aside from winding up the monkey and watching it play the drum, there's not much else a child can do with it, besides break it at some point. The lack of affordance an object provides limits the degree of co-creation possible. High-affordance objects usually lead to repeat usage because they provide sustainable experiences. Low-affordance objects quickly become boring. Think of the toys you played with most as a child, and you'll most likely realize they were high on affordance. They provided you with a lot of play options.

Affordance is related to customization. High affordance in an experience makes customization more likely and easier to achieve. There are two strategies for increasing the affordance of an experience. The first is to build more choices into the experience, but this approach comes with its own set of problems. There is a limit to the number of options consumers find useful before they become overwhelmed. Anyone who has shopped for orange juice has experienced choice overload when perusing orange juice permutations based on combinations of pulp-processing techniques and nutritional add-ins. To find the exact combination you want is time consuming. You must carefully read each label to identify your preferred type. Choices work best when just a few options are offered and their differences are distinct and recognizable. Simply increasing the number of choices does not offer customers the customized solution they're looking for, and so they end up settling for the closest fit to their needs.[11]

The second strategy is to increase the number of options within an experience. One way to do this is to be less definitive about the function of objects. In the design of playground equipment, for example, you can choose the degree of specificity. Think about the animals on springs that children like to ride in playgrounds. You could decide to design the equipment using a specific animal with a seat—a horse, for instance. Or, you could put a nondescript seat on the spring, thereby allowing children to use their imagination to decide whether they are

riding an animal or a spaceship. Putting a specific animal on the spring reduces the affordance of the playground equipment.

The number of interactive options within an experience or associated with a product can be increased by good design. Compare a common penknife with a Swiss Army knife. The former has one or two blades, whereas the latter has blades plus many more tools, allowing for more uses with the same basic knife configuration. It takes several box wrenches to equal one crescent wrench, which offers more affordance—it will work on more than one-size nut.

Today there is a tendency to use technology as a substitute for human interaction. The result is experiences and products with decreasing affordance, when the most desirable outcome is to increase affordance. Because of computer-driven programming, toy manufacturers can now offer toys with many play options. Here the problem of affordance is to make sure that the technology creates multiple interactive options for the child to do something—to be the cause of or participate in an act—rather than simply to watch the toy operate. Manufacturing a toy monkey with a computer chip that enables it to play three drum songs rather than one is not implementing useful user-focused affordance. Designers must use technology to increase affordance for the child, not to reduce it.

Another major impediment to affordance is developing rules, regulations, and management policies that restrict choices. Bob once read a *Ziggy* cartoon in which Ziggy was going to a public park. It was so long ago, Bob cannot find the original version to cite it, but what follows is the gist of the cartoon. Upon arriving in the park Ziggy was greeted by signs similar to the following: "Keep Off the Grass," "No Rollerblading," "Do Not Walk on the Grass," "No Swimming," and finally, "This Is YOUR PARK—Enjoy It—Your Park Commission!" When you design an experience, every rule you implement restricts choices and thereby affordance. Keep rules to a minimum, and make sure they enhance rather than impede the experience.

Affordance built into an experience by design can solve the problem of customization because multiple interactive options are present for the customer's taking. Customers can interact with the object or in the environment in multiple ways with no other intervention or provisions needed from the experience designer or stager. The most popular video games, for example, offer lots of interactive possibilities for the gamer. Video game designers try hard to build in affordance. But consider this irony: contrast the affordance available to the person

playing the game with the affordance available to the game designer who is programming the game for the computer. The programmer has much more affordance than the player. As an experience designer, you need to develop a sense of how to build affordance into your experiences so that you can build in multiple interactive possibilities for the participant rather than restricting them.

Co-creation and affordance are ways to facilitate opportunities for engagement. As you work through the design of each touchpoint, we encourage you to consider whether co-creation might help enhance the experience you're hoping to provide. Remember also that certain experience types are more conducive to co-creation than others. For example, prosaic experiences are not usually rich in co-creation or affordance. Section 5 of the touchpoint template addresses co-creation and asks you to indicate with a circle or dash mark on a high-to-low continuum how much co-creation you want to enable in the touchpoint. You then can provide brief details on what co-creation will look like for this touchpoint. This is a great space in which to make notes on how you might increase affordance for co-created touchpoints.

Transitions

Details make or break experiences. What sets great experience designers apart from good ones is their attention to detail. We've spent this whole chapter discussing details related to touchpoints, but we still need to consider the space between touchpoints. This is a space that is often overlooked. We're talking about transitions—the movement of people either spatially or cognitively from one touchpoint to another. Touchpoint transitions aren't necessarily very interesting, and sometimes they are not needed at all. This is why they're often overlooked, but they are the glue that binds an experience together. Accounting for and designing transitions does not take much time. But the space between touchpoints should be examined to determine whether a designed transition is needed. To complete section 7 of the touchpoint template, follow these steps:

1. Identify whether the transition is implicit or explicit. Is the transition obvious, or does it need additional explanation or direction? For example, you could think about each band playing at a music

festival as a separate touchpoint. The transition between bands is implicit because the audience does not need to be instructed to do anything to make the transition happen. A transition is explicit if the participants will need instruction on how to move from one touchpoint to the next. If you determine that the transition is implicit, you're finished and can move onto the next touchpoint. If it's explicit, you need to complete step 2.

2. Identify the outcome and intervention associated with the transition. This is the same process you completed for the touchpoint. Transitions happen quickly, so you need to have only one outcome and one intervention. For example, on a recent cruise Bob went to St. Petersburg, Russia. The day began onboard ship in the lounge, where groups were assigned to specific buses. Then passengers had to move from the ship, through Russian customs, and finally onto their waiting bus. The most critical point of this transition was going through customs. The cruise staff members, who were not allowed in the customs area, did three things to ensure a smooth transition. They released the group for each bus together so that the whole cohort began their journey at the same time, they had a highly visible staff member stationed at the entrance to customs to answer questions and help keep the groups together, and another staff member stood at the customs exit to reassemble groups and direct them to their waiting bus. Considering they had about 300 people to transition, the process went very well.

After completing these steps, you are finished designing the transition. As mentioned, it doesn't take much time, but seamless, well-executed transitions clearly communicate to your participants that this is a well-designed, intentional experience.

A Touchpoint Template for a New Employee Onboarding Experience

To help you better visualize what the touchpoint template looks like in action, let's walk through a short example. To anchor this thought exercise, imagine you are designing a new onboarding experience for employees in your company. You've already created your experience

map and have identified the critical touchpoints and the sequence needed to welcome and orient new employees. Now you must design each touchpoint in detail. Similar events fail when designers stop after developing the experience map and do not give sufficient design attention to each touchpoint.

For our example, we're going to look specifically at the touchpoint titled "registration." This touchpoint begins when employees walk up to the registration table and interact with one of your staff members, who will be registering new employees for the training. As a side note, the new employee's expectations and mood could have been influenced by how you conducted the anticipation phase of this experience with a letter, e-mail, or phone call informing the individual of the employee intake process. Based on how well you created anticipation and influenced expectations, the new employees could be excited and looking forward to onboarding; they could simply be neutral, with no expectations; or they could be dreading the experience. Such is the power of intentionally designing experience phases.

Since you have made it this far in the book and know how important the anticipation phase is, we'll assume you did a great job preparing employees for the experience. Now let's identify the information you need to complete the template and walk you through the task. Figure 7.3 provides an example of what a completed template would look like.

What follows is a detailed breakdown of each section of the touchpoint template in figure 7.3:

TEMPLATE HEADING

- **Touchpoint #3** (The first two touchpoints might involve participants reading the e-mail they received informing them of this event and arriving at the event location.)
- **Title**—Registration
- **Experience Type**—You want this to be a mindful experience. There is some information your participants need to receive when they register. However, you want this to be a quick and easy touchpoint, so it doesn't need to be memorable.
- **Desired Reaction**—When creating the experience map, you identified the following reactions for this touchpoint: "These people are friendly," "I am excited to get started working here," and "I know today's schedule for training."

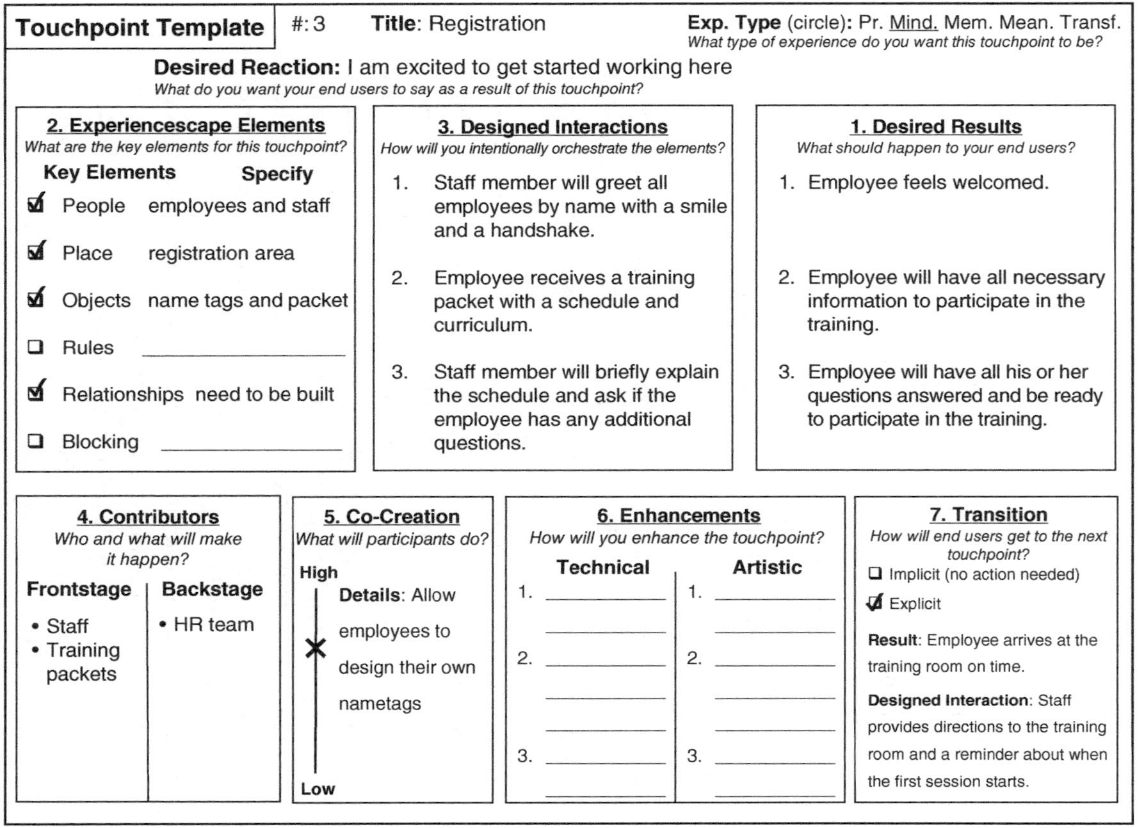

Figure 7.3 Touchpoint template example.

NUMBERED TEMPLATE BOXES

1. **Desired Results**—You now need to identify the results necessary to facilitate the desired reactions and then pinpoint the interventions that will produce these results. Here are some examples that are applicable to this touchpoint:
   - Employee feels welcomed.
   - Employee will have all necessary information to participate in the training.
   - Employee will have all his or her questions answered and be ready to participate in the training.
2. **Experiencescape Elements**—Although all elements will be present in each touchpoint, some are usually more salient than others to creating the intended reaction(s), and these should be the focus of your design. You will be able to pull some of this information from the front- and backstage contributor section (section 4) of the touchpoint template. Here's our perspective on the salience of each experiencescape element for this touchpoint (we've bolded the elements we feel are most salient for this touchpoint) along with some preliminary designed-interaction thoughts:
   - **People**—This includes the new employees, the registration staff, and their interactions with each other. You can also think about people who influence the touchpoint but are not present, like the new employees' supervisors; the new employees' families, who are probably excited for them to start a new job; or the company's human resources (HR) team who designed the training. Registration is a straightforward educational experience touchpoint within this training experience, so we're going to keep it simple.
   - **Place**—Because one of the desired reactions is "these people are friendly," you want the registration space to have a friendly feeling. To design this element, you would visualize walking through the place and evaluate it using the five senses to think of things you could do to make it contribute to the desired reaction. For example, the registration area should have good lighting and look professional.
   - **Objects**—The key objects for this touchpoint are the training packets to be distributed to employees and the signs indicating

that this is the registration area. There should be a conspicuous welcome sign, and if there is an important corporate logo or saying, such as a value statement or mission statement, it should be posted as well.

- Rules—This is a straightforward touchpoint. General rules of public decorum and civility apply, so we don't need to explicitly focus on them.
- **Relationships**—We know that these individuals are new employees who most likely don't have pre-existing relationships with current employees. Relationship building can be accomplished in several ways. You can have current employees or supervisors from the divisions involved come to welcome new employees. Or you can create mechanisms for the new hires to get acquainted so that they feel as if they know a colleague.
- Blocking—This simple touchpoint requires minimal blocking. The signage will direct people to the registration and training areas, and the training packets will explain the schedule for the rest of the day.

3. **Designed Interactions**—This is where you decide how to intentionally orchestrate the key experiencescape elements to produce the desired results:
    - Staff member will greet all employees by name with a smile and a handshake. If you really want a "wow," get registration staff to look at pictures of the new employees to become sufficient familiar to greet them by name when they arrive.
    - Employee receives a training packet with a schedule and curriculum.
    - Staff member will briefly explain the schedule and ask if the employee has any additional questions.
4. **Contributors**—For this touchpoint, the following contributors (people and things) were identified:
    - Frontstage—The staff running the registration table and the training packets, which include a schedule and the training curriculum.
    - Backstage—The HR team who developed the training packet materials and trained the registration table staff.
5. **Co-creation**—You decide that this touchpoint could benefit from a degree of co-creation to help facilitate the reaction of "I'm excited to start working here." Accordingly, you make a mark on

the co-creation high-to-low continuum and then start thinking about how to create opportunities for increased co-creation. Let's consider how name tags might be an opportunity for co-creation in this touchpoint. You could have preprinted, professional-looking name tags for attendees, or you could allow attendees to create their own IDs. Although this may seem to be a minor detail, how you handle it will send different messages. Premade name tags would help reinforce the professional nature of the workplace, whereas allowing people to create their own may provide an opportunity to break the ice and help people express their personality. You could even provide supplies for people to customize their name tags with the promise of awards for the best-designed name tags. Make sure the intervention aligns with the intended results. We hope this example shows you how co-creation can add energy and increase engagement in almost any touchpoint. You can also see how your ideas about co-creation may cause you to go back to modify some of your designed interactions, and that's perfectly okay. Design is an iterative process based on insights gained as you visualize and then stage the planned experience.

6. **Enhancements**—There are many things you can do to enhance the overall experience. More to come on these in chapter 9.
7. **Transition**—Because the transition to the next touchpoint involves employees walking to a different location, you decide that an explicit transition is needed. The desired outcome is that "the new employee arrives at the training room on time." The intervention is that "registration staff member provides directions to the training room and reminds the new employee about when the first session starts."

There you have it, the touchpoint template in action. After completing the templates for each touchpoint along a journey, you will have a very clear idea of what you want to have happen and how you're going to stage the experience. You'll also have a written plan that can be shared with others—few experiences are staged by one person. The collection of touchpoint templates that make up the macroexperience enables you to share the experience plan with the staging team, making sure there is clear communication about the experience and the role each team member will play. Think of the experience map as a roadmap to your desired destination, and your touchpoint templates as detailed

directions about how to get there. To provide you with another example of the touchpoint template in action, in chapter 10 we've included completed touchpoint templates for a product-driven experience.

Summary: A Comprehensive Experience Prototype

By implementing the recommended processes of experience mapping and touchpoint design, you will have in your possession a detailed design and staging plan for your experience. You will have carefully thought about your participants, how you want them to proceed through and react to each aspect of your experience, and how to turn them into co-creators. You will have created a prototype for the experience you hope to provide. You can now test it further or wait to embellish it with two additional sets of techniques we will introduce in chapters 8 and 9.

Before we wrap up this chapter, we want to suggest one other possible application for experience maps and touchpoint templates. We have discussed their use in this book primarily for design purposes, but experience maps and touchpoint templates can also be used to deconstruct existing experiences. We encourage you to take an experience you already provide and create an experience map and corresponding touchpoint templates to help you better understand what your experience offering currently looks like. We promise that you'll gain some interesting insights that will help you identify areas ripe for redesign and improvement. Sometimes deconstructing experiences is the first step in making them better. We think the oft-quoted statement attributed to Pablo Picasso that "every act of creation is first an act of destruction" applies well to redesigning existing experiences and believe that using experience maps and touchpoint templates will help you more effectively engage in this process.

With an experience map in hand, you are one step closer to staging an experience for your intended participants. It's important to recognize that by offering an experience to others, you are in essence inviting them to embark on a journey you have designed for them. Journeys, of many shapes and sizes, form the structure of almost all stories. Accordingly, experience designers should recognize and embrace their role as experiential storytellers. In the next chapter we're going to take a deep dive into the world of storytelling to show you why you need to think like a storyteller when designing experiences.

PART THREE

Creating Great Experiences

Enhancements and Examples

YOU NOW UNDERSTAND experiences as unique behavioral phenomena and have learned how to design them at the macro- and microexperience levels. In this section, we add to your experience design skillset with more techniques to enhance your designing abilities and the experience designs that result. We first look at the role storytelling can play in experience design and how you can build experience narratives to make your participants heroes. Then we discuss various technical and artistic factors you may consider applying to enhance your experience designs. We then conclude with a chapter demonstrating how experience design can be used to guide product development and how it is currently used to inform corporate strategies in several leading businesses.

CHAPTER EIGHT

The Stories We Tell

Building Drama in Your Experiences

"It was the best of times, it was the worst of times . . ."[1]

"In a hole in the ground there lived a hobbit."[2]

"A long time ago in a galaxy far, far away . . ."[3]

EVERYONE LOVES A good story. We enjoy being drawn into stories populated with interesting characters we come to care about or despise. Stories provide access to interesting places and people. They evoke emotion. They teach us about ourselves. They help us see the world in new ways. Great stories draw us in and lead us on a journey filled with new and unexpected elements. Certain stories resonate with each of us on a personal level. Mat loves *Peace Like a River* and *To Kill a Mockingbird*, among others. Bob's favorites include *The Hunt for Red October* and *Huckleberry Finn*.

In a world where experiences matter, people are expecting more than a transactional relationship with companies. C. K. Prahalad and Venkat Ramaswamy, business professors at the University of Michigan, suggest that companies need to create experience environments for their customers to engage in rather than just providing prepackaged goods

and services.[4] People want experiences with beginnings, middles, and endings. They want experiences that place them as actors in compelling stories that lead them on journeys toward desirable end destinations.

There are multiple mediums through which stories are told, including the written word, oral storytelling, movies, and plays. Experiences are also a storytelling medium. Although designing and delivering experiences is not always described as a storytelling process, we think it should be. The best experiences offer participants a chance to play a participatory role in an unfolding story. Do you know what type of story your experiences are telling your customers?

We want to introduce you to some ideas from the world of storytelling that can help you design more compelling experiences. In this chapter, we're going to discuss several storytelling topics, including why stories matter, the power of the narrative structure, how to make your end users heroes, and the role of backstories in experience design. Let's get started. It was a dark and stormy night . . . just kidding!

Why Stories Matter

In her book *The Power of Meaning: Creating a Life That Matters*, Emily Esfahani Smith makes the case for four primary sources of meaning in our lives: "belonging, purpose, storytelling, and transcendence."[5] Smith explains why storytelling makes the cut:

> Our storytelling impulse emerges from a deep-seated need all humans share: the need to make sense of the world. We have a primal desire to impose order on disorder—to find the signal in the noise. . . . We are constantly taking pieces of information and adding a layer of meaning to them; we couldn't function otherwise. Stories help us make sense of the world and our place it.[6]

People are already primed to tell stories about themselves and others, to tell about the experiences they have, so why not intentionally structure the experiences you design around stories? Remember The Color Run Event Model introduced in chapter 6? Step 2 in the model asks, "What do you want customers to say?" Another way to phrase this question is, "What stories do you want customers to tell about your experience?"

Brian Solis describes the moment customers start telling other people stories about their experiences as the ultimate moment of truth.[7] This retelling to others of what happened during the experience represents the culmination of the participants' experience journey and your design journey. The stories that people tell others about the experiences you provide have a profound influence on the life cycle of your experiences. In a world where one customer's story can potentially reach thousands and even millions through social media, you need to proactively and intentionally ensure that your designed experiences tell their own compelling stories.

A cynic might see this suggestion as license for manipulating people into parroting a prepackaged message, but this is not the case. The experience economy has ushered in an era of high experience literacy. If your experiences allow for co-creation, each participant will have had a slightly different experience. When we defined experiences in chapter 1, we explained that experiences arise out of interactions between participants and the designed elements of the experience. Customers are usually quick to recognize experiences that seem forced or unauthentic. The best experience designers use authentic stories that resonate with participants to guide the design of their macroexperiences.

Have you ever made a piñata or other papier-mâché creation? Piñata-making skills are not a prerequisite for being an experience designer, but the process does provide a helpful analogy for how stories can help shape experiences. To build a piñata you create a framework, on which you drape and wrap strips of paper that have been dipped into a mixture of glue and water or flour and water. Although the framework is eventually covered by paper, the framework is what gives the piñata shape and meaning. Imagine that instead of a piñata at your child's birthday party you simply had a pile of wet strips of papier-mâché. This would evoke many reactions different than those you would expect if you had an actual piñata. A pile of papier-mâché is going to elicit reactions like "Gross, what's that?" A real piñata, in contrast, will elicit reactions like "Look, it's a cowboy!" or "Cool, it's a rocket ship!" The framework covered with paper creates a structure that tells a story.

Narrative frameworks for experiences provide form and convey meaning to your end users, much as cardboard frameworks for piñatas provide form and convey meaning to kids at birthday parties. Think of an experience map as a long strip of papier-mâché. As it lies there flat

on the table, uniform and two-dimensional, it doesn't engender much excitement for the experience it's outlining. But if we have a story to wrap that experience map around, it becomes three-dimensional. It has form and structure that invites curiosity and guided interpretation.

Great stories make great experiences. They are what differentiate a generic amusement park from a Disney theme park. Strip the stories away from Disneyland or Disneyworld, and the magic is gone. The stories and the attention given to making them come to life is why Disney theme parks are unique. Everything about these parks is built on stories that people already know. People watch Disney movies and then go to Disney theme parks to experience attractions that immerse them in these same stories. No one had any idea what Walt Disney was trying to do when he started talking about building Disneyland. Devin Leonard and Christopher Palmeri, in an article about Disney theme parks for *Bloomberg Businessweek*, wrote about the difficulty that Walt Disney had in trying to explain his vision for story-driven experiences:

> When Walt Disney set out to create Disneyland in the early 1950s, the modern theme park didn't exist. There were plenty of roadside attractions with roller coasters and Ferris wheels, but what Disney had in mind was so radical he had trouble articulating it to consultants and bankers. Even his wife thought he was crazy. "Nobody really knew what he was talking about," says Margaret King, director of the Center for Cultural Studies & Analysis, a firm in Philadelphia that has done park research for Disney and SeaWorld Entertainment Inc. "The closest he could come was to say that he was going to try to sort of cast his films in 3D form, so it was a movie you could walk around in."[8]

Disney was trying to tell people he was going to design experiences built on well-known stories, but no one had done something like that before. It obviously turned out to be a good idea.

Although Disney has long held the lion's share of the market when it comes to theme parks, Universal Studios gained ground on Disney with the opening of The Wizarding World of Harry Potter in its Orlando theme park. Universal Studios recognized that the company needed its own broadly recognized stories to compete with Disney in the theme-park space. The richness and fidelity of the experience provided in The Wizarding World of Harry Potter when it opened in 2010 boosted attendance to Universal Studios by almost 70 percent.[9] As Leonard

and Palmeri discuss in their article, Disney and Universal Studios are locked in a fierce theme-park market-share battle in which billions of dollars are at stake.[10] This contest between two very powerful organizations is pertinent to our discussion in this chapter because at its core is a fight over stories and who owns the rights to bring them to life as immersive experiences.

Universal Studios has cut into Disney's theme-park dominance using the power of Harry Potter. Disney is readying a narrative counterstrike with the opening of new lands at Disney World and Disneyland built on the stories of *Avatar* and *Star Wars*, respectively. This clash of corporate titans powerfully illustrates the importance of stories in designing experiences. Although you're not likely in the position to purchase the rights to Harry Potter stories to frame your next experience, it doesn't mean you can't use storytelling to enrich your design process. Stories provide rich, already familiar contexts in which you can design experiences. Using pre-existing stories can serve as an excellent starting point for designing experiences, but so too can using the standard narrative framework that undergirds almost all stories.

Dramatic Structure

For some of you, this discussion might seem like a flashback to a ninth-grade English class, but stick with us because your ninth-grade English teacher unknowingly held the key to some great experience design insights. In 1863 Gustav Freytag, a German novelist, wrote *Die Technik des Dramas*, in which he proposed the following five phases of traditional stories: exposition, rising action, climax, falling action, dénouement.[11] Although there are, of course, stories that don't follow this structure, many do. We also think that Freytag's five phases of dramatic structure provide an excellent experience design rubric. If you reflect on some of the best experiences you've had, they can probably be broken down into these five phases. As an example, let's examine how we could use Freytag's five phases to analyze a cruise experience. Table 8.1 provides a definition for each phase along with an example of how you could use it to deconstruct a cruise ship experience.

As you build experience maps, keep Freytag's five phases in mind. Are you creating experiences that give sufficient attention to each of the five phases? Do you have a climax touchpoint? Do you provide

TABLE 8.1
Five Phases of Dramatic Structure

Phase	Description	Example
Exposition	The introduction where all necessary information about the setting, characters, and so on is shared with the audience	Booking the cruise and receiving information about the cruise along with the onboarding and orientation process
Rising Action	All events that lead up to the climax. This phase tends to be the longest part of a story.	The bulk of your cruise experience (e.g., onboard activities, dining, shore excursions)
Climax	The moment to which the story has been building, often a turning point for good or bad depending on the type of story	Most cruises have one or two highlight experiences. This could be a formal dinner or ball on the last night, or a signature port of call.
Falling Action	The story begins to wrap up as the impact of the climax plays out.	This phase includes returning to the home port and disembarking.
Dénouement	The final resolution if the story is a comedy, or the final fall if it's a tragedy	You return home from the cruise and back to your regular life laden with memories and memorabilia to share with family and friends.

Source: Gustav Freytag, *Freytag's Technique of the Drama: An Exposition of Dramatic Composition and Art*, trans. Elias J. MacEwan (Chicago: S. C. Griggs, 1895).

an adequate and satisfactory resolution? The five phases are a great measuring stick with which to judge the robustness of the experiences you're designing. Although each experience is unique, using these five phases across all your experiences can help you build additional drama into your experiences and thereby elicit more participant interest and engagement. Thinking of your participants as characters within stories you are creating can be a powerful change in thinking for you as an experience designer. Just as theme-park designers want to create immersive, story-driven experiences for patrons, you too should strive to create immersive experiences for your participants. In fact, you might even consider making them the heroes of the story.

The Hero's Journey

As previously discussed in this chapter, humans are hardwired to think narratively. In his seminal work *The Hero with a Thousand Faces*, the mythologist Joseph Campbell proposed that stories across time and cultures share a similar structure.[12] He used the term *monomyth* to suggest that all stories have their origins in one common myth or narrative structure, which he called "the hero's journey." Chris Vogler, while working on story development at Disney studios in the 1980s, synthesized Joseph Campbell's work into a seven-page white paper that became widely read throughout the screenwriting world and remains influential today.[13]

George Lucas was a disciple of Campbell and has talked about how he intentionally used the hero's journey to craft the narrative for *Star Wars*.[14] When you review the phases of the hero's journey, it quickly becomes apparent that almost any story you can think of, from comedy to tragedy to children's bedtime stories, fits into its structure. Table 8.2 provides an overview of the twelve steps of the hero's journey as summarized by Vogler. To show a contemporary example of how the hero's journey pops up everywhere, in the second column we include a descriptive narrative of Google's Super Bowl ad entitled "Parisian Love."[15]

As you think about the steps shown in table 8.2, what stories come to mind? We've already mentioned *Star Wars*, so you can't count that one. Some other easy ones include *The Lord of the Rings* and all the Marvel movies. Try out this little challenge to test Campbell's claim: Think of the last movie you watched or novel you read and analyze how well it lines up with these steps. Not all stories fit perfectly, but almost any story you can think of will exhibit elements of the hero's journey.

What does this have to do with experience design? Everything, we think. The hero's journey gives you a template to design experiences in which your participants become the heroes. Again, you don't have to cover every step of the journey in the experience you're designing. But when designing your experiences, doesn't it make sense to use a framework that for thousands of years has served as the structure for stories?

What does this look like in practice? Consider the ad "Parisian Love," which we broke down in table 8.2. It is a great example of a complete hero's journey told in only fifty-two seconds. What's even more amazing is that the only thing you see during the entire ad is

TABLE 8.2
Steps of the Hero's Journey

Phases	Description	Example
The Ordinary World	The hero, uneasy, uncomfortable, or unaware, is introduced sympathetically so that the audience can identify with the situation or dilemma.	We meet the hero as he searches the internet using Google.
The Call to Adventure	Something shakes up the situation—the hero must face the beginnings of change.	The hero searches about study abroad programs in Paris.
Refusal of the Call	The hero feels the fear of the unknown and tries to turn away from the adventure.	
Meeting with the Mentor	The hero comes across a seasoned traveler of the world who gives him or her training, equipment, or advice that will help on the journey.	The mentor in this story is the Google search engine that provides the hero with important information and encouragement to embark on an adventure to Paris.
Crossing the Threshold	The hero commits to leaving the Ordinary World and entering a new region with unfamiliar rules and values.	You hear the sounds of an airport and planes taking off, which signals that the hero has heeded the call to adventure.
Tests, Allies, and Enemies	The hero is tested and sorts out allegiances in the Special World.	Over the next twenty seconds, the hero faces a series of challenges (e.g., language barriers, searching for a gift) involved in courting a Parisian girl. His wise mentor, the Google search engine, helps him navigate these challenges.
Approach	The hero and his or her newfound allies prepare for the major challenge in the Special World.	We see the hero, now having fallen in love, searching for tips about long-distance relationships.

TABLE 8.2 (*Continued*)

Phases	Description	Example
The Ordeal	Near the middle of the story, the hero enters a central space in the Special World and confronts death or faces his or her greatest fear. Out of the moment of death comes a new life.	The searching shifts to focus on finding jobs in Paris and booking a flight back to Paris.
The Reward	The hero takes possession of the treasure won by facing death. There may be celebration, but there is also danger of losing the treasure again.	The hero, now back in Paris, searches for churches in Paris and we hear wedding bells in the background.
The Road Back	About three-fourths of the way through the story, the hero is driven to complete the adventure and to leave the Special World to be sure the treasure is brought home.	
The Resurrection	At the climax, the hero is severely tested once more on the threshold of home. He or she is purified by a last sacrifice, another moment of death and rebirth, but on a higher and more complete level.	The hero has become a married man living in Paris.
Return with the Elixir	The hero returns home, bearing some element of the treasure that has the power to transform the world just as the hero has been transformed.	The hero's final Google search is "how to assemble a crib," and we hear a baby crying in the background.

Source: Christopher Vogler, "A Practical Guide to Joseph Campbell's *The Hero with a Thousand Faces*," *The Writer's Journey*, 1985, para. 2–13, http://www.thewritersjourney.com/hero%27s_journey.htm#Memo.

the Google search engine in action, with some accompanying sound effects and barely audible dialog. Despite these constraints, you still experience the unfolding of a compelling heroic journey in under a minute. The URL for the ad is included in the endnotes for this chapter, so you can check it out yourself. We're confident that you can find ways to weave the hero's journey into your designed experiences. At a minimum, thinking about your participants as heroes helps you remember that you're designing the experiences to meet their needs, not your own. We encourage you to use the hero's journey framework in your own experience design work. We feel confident that doing so will lead you to some interesting perspectives as you do your work.

Front Story or Backstory?

When you read a book or watch a play or movie, what you are experiencing is the front story. This is the part of the story the novelist, screenwriter, or playwright shares with you, the audience. It is the story that leads you through the five dramatic phases. In almost all instances, there is also an untold backstory behind the front story. The backstory consists of all the stories and information that support the front story. Authors will often have extensive backstory descriptions of characters and settings that they draw on to create the front story. Backstories are sometimes revealed when authors are interviewed about their work and are asked questions about characters or plots. In some instances, backstories later become front stories. These are called origin stories, a staple element of most superhero movies.

If backstories are such a helpful tool for writers as they create rich stories, it seems reasonable to suggest that backstories could also help in the design of experiences. You don't have to look too hard to find examples of experience designers using backstories to create experiences. As we've already discussed in this chapter, Disney's theme parks and Universal Studios' Wizarding World are successful because of their backstories. Sometimes a backstory can be as simple as a well-established theme (e.g., holidays, pirates, medieval times) that allows participants to immediately bring their memories of previous encounters with the theme into the experience you've designed.[16]

Backstories can act as a facilitating constraint for experience designers. Let us explain what we mean with this counterintuitive phrase,

"facilitating constraint."[17] Designing experiences is a creative act, one you should initially approach with an open mind regarding the potential directions the process might take you; the limitless options they facilitate can quickly feel overwhelming. Luckily, you usually have some externally imposed constraints such as a preselected target audience, a budget, or a venue; one or more of these preset conditions will limit your options. These constraints help narrow the feasible options and help you focus the design process on what is practically possible. Constraints can impede innovation if too much focus is placed on them early in the design process, but adding facilitating constraints such as themes and backstories as your initial design emerges can be helpful. Let us share a few real-world examples to demonstrate what we mean.

The Polynesian Cultural Center Story

The Polynesian Cultural Center (PCC) in Laie, Hawaii, is one of the top tourist attractions on the island of Oahu.[18] The PCC's forty-two acres are divided into eight areas, each focusing on a different Polynesian island. In 2015, the PCC finished a seven-year renovation project. Part of this project includes a new area called the Hukilau Marketplace with shops paying homage to the early history and culture of the local community.[19] Mike Lee, president of MLD Worldwide, the design firm that oversaw the entire PCC renovation project from 2008 to 2015, cited the creation of backstories as a key step in designing the marketplace.[20] The design of each shop was guided by a detailed backstory about 1950s life in Laie.

The IKEA Story

Another example of an experience design backstory comes from IKEA. As you probably already know, shopping at IKEA is very different from most shopping experiences. The IKEA experience involves not only the build-it-yourself nature of the furniture but also a unique customer journey. When you visit an IKEA store, instead of walking up and down aisles of merchandise you embark on a journey through fully furnished living rooms, dining rooms, kitchens, and bathrooms. Doing this almost gives you the feeling that you're walking through someone's house, and in a way, you are.

When IKEA designers create the layouts for their showrooms, they often create backstories about the families who "live" there.[21] These backstories include details about who lives in each room, what they do for work, and what hobbies they enjoy. The richness of these backstories helps the designers create spaces that feel authentic because they have been designed to reflect the personality of their fictional occupants. IKEA's designers have done an excellent job of creating personas of these individuals.

We encourage you to consider creating a backstory the next time you set out to design an experience. Take time to think about the story behind the experience you're designing. Scott Lukas, in his book *The Immersive Worlds Handbook*, details the process whereby tangible immersive worlds like theme parks and restaurants are designed.[22] When you write a backstory to kick-start your design process, you are creating an intangible world that will provide a context for your experience. The backstory is the unspoken story from which rich experiences emerge.

Summary: The End

The story—that is, chapter 8—is now ending. We've covered a lot of content, from *Avatar* to IKEA showrooms. We feel strongly about stories. Great experiences are often built on great stories. We encourage you to embrace the role of storyteller as you design experiences. What stories do you want to tell your participants? What stories do you want your participants to tell others? Doing this well will make you an experience design hero. Stories provide useful drama for the experiences you will create. Sometimes using a pre-existing story line will get you out of a thinking block and get you moving forward again, even if you do not use the story that got you started.

We've come a long way since chapter 1, but we have a few more topics to cover before we're done. If we were to compare the progress we've made to this point to the act of making a cake, our freshly baked cake would be cooling on the counter and we would be ready for frosting and decorating—the final touches. In the next chapter we discuss the technical and artistic factors you need to consider as you finalize your experience designs.

CHAPTER NINE

Techniques for Enhancing Experiences

AS MENTIONED AT the conclusion of chapter 8, designing experiences bears similarities to making a cake. Both processes involve steps that must be completed in the correct order. To make a cake, you mix the batter, bake the cake, and then decorate it. For many people, the most engaging and rewarding aspect of the process—aside from eating the cake, of course—is frosting and decorating. The cake serves as the canvas on which you give expression to your creativity. The decorative adornments of a cake are what people initially see and respond to. These decorations are why so many people watch cake and cupcake competitions on TV—they want to see the amazing creations of expert bakers.

Even though many bakers may admit a preference for the decoration phase of cake making, they would not discount the importance of creating a moist, delicious cake as the foundational act of making a cake. Although an externally beautiful cake makes a great initial impression, positive feelings about the cake would quickly dissipate if it tasted awful. Making a great cake requires fully engaging in all the necessary steps, from mixing ingredients to baking the cake to placing the last carefully crafted fondant cake topper.

When designing experiences, you may also be tempted to jump right into working on the types of finishing touches we're introducing in this chapter. We like to call these experience enhancements; they're analogous to the frosting and decorating stages of making a cake. When correctly applied, they can make an ordinary experience or an ordinary cake extraordinary, but only if the underlying experience or cake is high quality to begin with. So, remember this analogy as we discuss enhancing experiences. If you follow the process of experience design thinking laid out in a previous chapter and diligently follow the other tools in the experience designer's toolkit, you will design excellent experiences. Yes, doing this takes time and attention, but it's worth it. This is what people who design great experiences do. After you move through the ideation, prototyping, and testing phases, you should then start thinking about adding the enhancements discussed in this chapter. If you do so, you will be rewarded with an experience that not only looks great but delivers desired outcomes as well.

This chapter also represents a transition of sorts from designing experiences to delivering them. Great experiences require both great design and great delivery. An amazing experience design can quickly become meaningless if the delivery is poor. In the academic literature, we call the match between experience design and delivery "implementation fidelity."[1] High implementation fidelity indicates the experience was delivered as designed; low implementation fidelity signals there were delivery gaps. Although the topic of experience delivery deserves its own standalone book, we believe this chapter is a good start to thinking about things you need to consider as you design experiences and prepare to deliver them.

Using figure skating, the work of B. Joseph Pine II and James H. Gilmore,[2] and various other customer service thinkers like Anantharanthan Parasuraman, Valarie Zeithaml, and Leonard L. Berry,[3] Bob worked with Gary Ellis to create a two-category experience-enhancements framework.[4] They described this framework as follows:

> In figure skating, judges evaluate the extent to which competitors execute specific skills correctly—technical performance. And, in a separate evaluation, they rate the competitors' creativity, beauty, and musical interpretation, for example, artistic performance. Consistent with that metaphor, the "technical performance" of professionals can be distinguished from their "artistic performance" in staging an encounter.[5]

The following sections provide an overview of selected technical and artistic factors. We realize that each section could be much longer, but not all permutations can be covered in a chapter.

Technical Factors

When you participate in an experience, you usually have a set of baseline expectations. For example, you expect the venue to be clean, the frontline staff to be courteous, and signage to be clear and informative. There are certain factors you expect to be properly executed; these are the technical factors, and they must be executed well or they will detract from your main purpose of providing a quality macroexperience. In the more common vernacular, technical factors are often referred to as the service elements of an experience. *Merriam-Webster* defines *service* as "useful labor that does not produce a tangible commodity."[6] A common favorite example of bad service is the Department of Motor Vehicles (DMV). The product you receive as a result of visiting the DMV, a driver's license, is satisfactory, but what you experience while obtaining it is often less than desirable. DMVs, probably because they operate as a monopoly, do not always pay adequate attention to the technical factors of the experience they offer. Most organizations cannot operate as a monopoly and are consequently likely to lose business if they provide poor experiences.

In the following sections, we will introduce the technical service factors most often associated with high-quality experiences (see table 9.1). These factors are drawn from a service-quality framework developed by Parasuraman and his colleagues.[7] Not all technical factors will be applicable for all experiences, so you will need to determine which are most important for the experiences you're designing.

You will notice that many of the technical factors listed in table 9.1 directly involve front-stage employees and the service attributes of an experience. As explained in our discussion of front- and backstage contributors in chapter 6, front-stage employees directly interact with end users. A front-stage employee can often singlehandedly redeem or derail an experience, depending on how the employee engages with participants. Although the technical factors we'll discuss are things you've probably thought about before, we believe that pulling all the elements together in one framework promotes systematic reflection on each

TABLE 9.1
Technical Factors Adapted in Part From Parasuraman, Zeithaml, and Berry

Communication	Necessary information about the experience is clearly communicated to end users.
Competence	Experience stagers have the requisite knowledge and skill to deliver the experience.
Courtesy	Experience stagers have a professional appearance and interact with participants in a professional manner.
Credibility	Experience stagers are perceived as trustworthy.
Recovery	Experience stagers can recover from an experience delivery error.
Reliability	The experience is delivered in a consistent and expected manner.
Responsiveness	Participant needs are quickly addressed.
Security	Customers feel emotionally and physically safe during the experience.
Tangibles	The physical elements of the experiencescape are high quality.

Source: Anantharanthan Parasuraman, Valarie A. Zeithaml, and Leonard L. Berry, "Servqual: A Multiple-Item Scale for Measuring Consumer Perceptions," *Journal of Retailing* 64, no. 1 (1988): 12.

element as you design and deliver an experience. Consider table 9.1 as a checklist for the technical or service delivery elements that serve as the foundation for high-quality experiences. We realize that each of these topics involves much more than we can include in this book, so we have focused on overviews and in some cases on errors we believe are made frequently.

Communication

Effective communication with participants is making sure you tell them enough to make their experience seamless but not so much that they become overwhelmed. Effective communication is not necessarily more communication, though often more communication is the solution to perceived communication problems. The test is, Did people understand what they need to know at this point in the experience? A general solution to this problem is to apportion the information on a need-to-know basis so that all the information is not given at one time.

To help you know when to provide specific information, make communication content and delivery an element of your experience map and touchpoint templates. This can help you make sure you're telling people what they need to know when they need to know it.

Signage is another important communication conduit that requires intentional attention. If you notice customers becoming disoriented or lost within an experiencescape, it's often because of inadequate signage. You should also consider the secondary messages your signage might convey. For example, a sign that reads "Staff Only" is much friendlier than one that reads "Keep Out," even though they both serve the same purpose. You may have seen signs in parking lots warning about the danger of people breaking into cars. Can you think of a different way to encourage people not to leave valuables in their car that doesn't have them starting off their experience being worried about crime in the area? Everything speaks, remember? Make sure the messages you communicate to participants clearly convey the information needed and also help facilitate the intended outcomes of the experience.

Competence

Are front-stage employees competent and well trained for their respective positions? Do they know the answers to questions participants are likely to ask? Are they able to complete their part of the experience journey in a timely and competent manner? Staff incompetence creates real frustration for participants. You have likely been involved in encounters where there are multiple service lines and you end up in a line that is held up because the person serving your line cannot complete some part of the transaction. So, that person must call on a fellow staff member from another line. Now two lines are held up. Sometimes this gets even worse, and numerous lines are held up because one staff member cannot complete a required task. The obvious solution to this dilemma is to have sufficient supervisory staff positioned so that they can immediately intervene and rectify problems that arise.

Inadequately trained sales associates are frequently frustrating. In many big-box stores, finding the right person to answer your specific question can be difficult because of the overwhelming number of products provided in the store. Most of the employees work at the checkout counter, and their expertise is in operating the cash register, not understanding features of merchandise. Having a well-trained staff

is a challenge if you experience a lot of turnover in your workforce. Often employers do not want to invest resources in training employees they will soon lose. But poorly trained employees are an obstacle to providing good experiences for customers. So, a suitable balance needs to be found to adequately serve the organization and its customers.

Courtesy

In many situations, microexperience interactions with front-stage employees have a significant influence on a participant's overall macroexperience. Front-stage employees can create experience peaks and fill in pits if they are correctly trained. There are several dimensions to consider when thinking about employee and participant interactions. First, are employees courteous to customers? Are customers treated as valuable individuals the organization hopes will return? Do customers believe their presence matters? For example, are customers greeted when they enter a store and also given an appropriate parting comment when they leave? Walgreen pharmacies for a time required each employee to complete transactions with the comment "Be well!"—a perfect summation of Walgreen's reason for existing as a company and its service to customers. Some theater venues have their ushers thank patrons for coming as the patrons leave the venue after a performance. Courtesy never goes out of style, and in many cases it doesn't take a big investment of time, just the right dialogue delivered at the right time.

Are employees appropriately friendly? Notice that we asked whether they are *appropriately* friendly; often employees are encouraged or trained to be inappropriately friendly. In some service encounters, a certain expected demeanor is lacking. For example, it's not always appropriate for young employees to address older customers by their first names, yet this often happens. In many experiences, customers are not expecting to create enduring friendships with front-stage employees. The interaction is a role relationship engaged in for a short time with no expectation for continuation—for instance, interactions with your waiter at a restaurant or a ticketing agent at the airport.

The need for security has made employee courtesy a daunting challenge for many venues because a customer's first encounter with the experience usually involves the security protocol and security personnel. This is so not only at airports but also at many large stadiums and venues. Unfortunately, employees involved in security do not generally

see themselves as members of the team providing a pleasant experience for customers; rather, they view their role as enforcement personnel. With appropriate training, however, it's possible for these individuals to embrace both roles. Mat recently took his family to Disneyland, where he noticed that the security personnel took it upon themselves to make the security line a positive experience. Knowing the thoroughness of Disney, they were likely trained to do so. Their actions ranged from engaging in friendly banter as they examined bags to encouraging everyone in line to cheer because they were almost in Disneyland.

How do you make sure that your front-stage employees are friendly and courteous? It seems obvious, but thinking about it and developing dialogues and scripts that send the intended messages are essential. You can't simply rely on hiring friendly people; you need to create an intentional culture of courtesy and train people accordingly. This is important for all employees as well as volunteers who interact directly with end users. Keep in mind The Color Run model discussed in chapter 6: if you know what you want your participants to say at various touchpoints along their journey, you can empower front-stage staff to think proactively about what they can do to facilitate the reactions desired.

Credibility

Do the actions and activities of front-stage staff instill trust in their abilities to meet guests' needs and correctly provide the experience intended? This is especially important in experiences that have some risk—outdoor adventure experiences, for example. Often a simple opening comment about how long someone has been working in a position or how frequently that staff member has visited a site can instill trust and allay concerns. To implement this, it's useful for staff to have a scripted opening dialogue that welcomes participants, instills confidence in the staff member's ability to operate the experience, and gives a preview of what is to come in the experience. Individuals who have had event-leadership training will know this, but some of your employees may not have had this training and will need to be taught.

Bob was once asked to help organize university commencement exercises. In previous years, there had been problems at the assembly site for students who were participating. Students were not paying attention to directions, and the faculty members were having trouble getting them in lines. The year before Bob's involvement, faculty had

tried to use megaphones to give instructions. He suggested that they instead initiate one-on-one contact with arriving students to greet them, introduce themselves, congratulate them on graduating, welcome them to commencement exercises, and tell them what they had to do to participate. This did not take long and worked well. Students were welcomed, saw that someone was in charge, and learned that there was a plan they had a part in to complete the event. Students who had already received the information felt responsible to pass it on to arriving students. In this case, providing the knowledge needed to participate in commencement exercises created credibility.

Recovery

Experiences are delivered and consumed concurrently; in this real-time production process, some errors invariably occur. When they do occur, how well do front-stage staff members recover from errors? Staff should be prepared to recover gracefully from mistakes that are anticipated and predictable. For example, in operations involving large crowds of families, it is predictable that there will be lost children. Is there a plan for how to handle this?

There is the famous case that occurred in 2017 when United Airlines forcibly reclaimed a seat from a passenger who was already on board the aircraft. It is a good example of inadequate anticipation of a predictable occurrence.[8] Didn't anyone anticipate that someone may resist giving up their seat once seated on board the aircraft? Evidently not! Even worse, the organization seemed unprepared to recover from the incident in the short run, thus dooming the airline to much bad publicity, a large financial settlement, and devaluation of United's stock.

Everyone has likely had a negative incident of some kind in a restaurant. Lost or incomplete orders and wrong charges, all are predictable errors that occur while operating a restaurant. Wait staff should be trained and prepared to recover from these predictable incidents. Ideally, problems never happen; but, as Murphy's law predicts, "anything that can go wrong, will go wrong." When there are irregularities, staff must be prepared to recover from them gracefully, and they should be given as much authority as needed to do so because successfully salvaging a mistake can win more customer loyalty than if the mistake had never occurred in the first place.[9]

Reliability

Reliability is assuring that what was promised is indeed delivered. Was the experience staged effectively to ensure that customer expectations are met and the designer's intended outcomes realized? Knowing the source of expectations helps ensure their delivery. Often experience designers create expectations in their program fliers or advertising campaign. These are expectations you know about.

But there can be expectations created elsewhere that you may not know about. Word-of-mouth recommendations from previous participants can create unknown and possibly unreal expectations. Individuals may have participated in a similar experience operated by another organization and assume that your operation will be the same. Or participants may have participated in a similar experience, like a lesson of golf, for example, and assume that your tennis lessons will be operated similarly.

Seth King, the vice president of field marketing for the outdoor gear brand Cotopaxi, notes that "the customer's perspective of your brand is cumulative."[10] He means that even if you've changed the experiences you provide, repeat participants will be coming with expectations drawn from their previous experiences, and you should be aware of what those are. The repeat customers may be disappointed that the experience was "not like it was the last time," although you think you improved it. Other companies can also set expectation benchmarks you may not know about but will be judged on anyway. If you've done your empathy homework, as outlined in chapter 5, you should be ready to deliver high levels of reliability and meet the expectations of your participants.

Responsiveness

Do front-stage employees react to participant requests promptly and appropriately? Responsiveness is often focused on dealing with situations in which routine procedure has failed and the customer must seek out an alternative. Other times it may be focused on situations in which the customer has a unique issue needing resolution. These scenarios are very likely to occur, so staff members should anticipate that they will and be prepared to deal with those that regularly do. We have all had the problem of trying to attract someone's attention for help. Staff members who are staging an experience must be

visible and available to participants. A staff member who is available is the participants' first need; a staff member who is trained and able to respond appropriately is their second. Too often customers must wait for a staff supervisor or someone with higher authority to respond to anything other than a routine occurrence. Operational policies must empower front-stage staff to resolve anticipated recurring problems so that they are dealt with quickly and thoroughly.

Responsiveness can be difficult in contexts where customers may have different notions about appropriate responsiveness, as, for example, in restaurants. To be available and responsive, waiters in some chain restaurants are trained to check back frequently with guests—so frequently, they are sometimes there to check on the first bite of food. Extreme levels of responsiveness can turn into undesirable hovering. Our own preference is for wait staff to be on call when needed but not to invade table conversation with a constant stream of questions and interruptions. Of course, other patrons may prefer the constant attentiveness. Getting this right can be difficult.

To improve responsiveness, some hotel chains now have a single number guests can dial if they have needs and questions. The operator at this number is usually empowered to obtain an immediate response, whether for housekeeping, bookkeeping, or maintenance. The hotel operator used to ask, "Which department would you like?" Now the operator makes the decision for you by determining which hotel department is the appropriate one to respond to your question; the customer no longer has to figure it out by dialing several different departments until the correct one is located.

Security

People have always had a basic need to feel secure. Today, there is an obviously heightened need to assure experience participants that they are secure—physically, socially, and emotionally. Unfortunately, some of the procedures needed to ensure security are physically invasive or take up time that could be used for the experience itself. Think creatively about ways you can keep people safe. Try to make them feel welcome and assured about safety at the same time. Think back to Mat's example of the security line personnel at Disneyland. That you must go through a security line to get into the "Happiest Place on Earth" seems ironic, but the cleanliness of the venue, the themed

music playing in the background, and the courtesy of the staff make the security line a positive anticipation phase experience, as opposed to a frustrating, anxiety-inducing one. This was achieved through good experience design.

It's also important that security procedures result in participants' feeling secure. Opinion varies about how much security the Transportation Security Administration (TSA) procedures achieve at airports. Well-publicized failures of TSA agents passing various tests of their procedures add to this skepticism. Current procedures are designed so that TSA personnel spend the same amount of time on each passenger rather than screening and spending more time on high-risk passengers. This approach also erodes support for and confidence in the process. The burden here for the experience designer is to develop security protocols that seem appropriate for the experience, take as little time as possible, and create a feeling of security through actual security rather than just the illusion of it. In today's world, there is no doubt that security is needed, and how it is implemented should be a positive part of each participant's experience journey, not a memorable negative part of the experience.

Tangibles

Tangibles are the physical elements of the venue and the environment where an experience is delivered. A first concern is selecting a venue appropriate for the intended experience. Are the physical layout and design of the venue appropriate for the experience being delivered? There are many obvious concerns regarding a facility, including adequate size, appropriate accessibility, sufficient seating, and so on. Is the venue clean, neat, and orderly? People prefer clean and neat facilities that are well designed. Is the venue comfortable in terms of temperature and humidity? Are sound levels of music or speaking presentations appropriate?

These days even manufacturing plants are kept as neat and clean as possible because this improves employee safety and satisfaction, as well as productivity. This is an issue that seems obvious but can inadvertently hinder a good experience. People expect tangibles to be in order, so there is usually no accolade if they are, but there is great discontent if they are not. Remember Buc-ee's bathrooms, a tangible aspect turned into a memorable touchpoint of the experience!

Artistic Factors

Whereas technical factors fall under the category of baseline service experience expectations, artistic factors (see table 9.2) are a collection of staging strategies drawn in large part from Pine and Gilmore.[11] These lend added and unexpected value to your experiences and help embellish an experience. You shouldn't attempt to use all artistic factors in every experience you design; rather, choose those that seem to best embellish specific experiences (i.e., they add to achieving the intended outcomes and are on theme). In the following sections we'll introduce each factor, describe it, and provide examples where each has contributed in a unique way to an experience. Again, obviously much more could be written about each.

Characterizing

Your experience needs to have a unique characterizing signature. The idea of characterizing experience-staging roles (e.g., employees at Disneyland are cast members, Best Buy Geek Squad employees are agents), an idea introduced by Pine and Gilmore,[12] can be applied to experiences themselves. How is participating in your experience different from participating in others that may be available? Airlines try very

TABLE 9.2
Artistic Factors

Characterizing	Ensuring your experiences have a recognizable, signature style
Customizing	Modifying experiences to meet the unique needs and desires of individual participants
Empathy	Providing attention to participants based on attempts to see the experience from their perspective
Experience Deepening	Intentionally designing all phases (anticipation, participation, reflection) of an experience
Memorializing	Creating touchpoints designed to produce memories for participants
Sensitizing	Considering all five senses when designing experiences
Theming	Using themes to guide the design of an experience

hard to provide a unique experience signature. Flying Southwest is different from flying American, for instance. Both companies have well-appointed airplanes that can take you to the same places. But there are signature differences, including the way they decorate the planes, the clientele they try to attract, the food they serve or don't serve, the onboard entertainment they provide, and whether they charge for checking luggage, as well as many other unique signature features that give each airline a distinct character.

Companies that offer outdoor adventure trips vary in the number of chores they expect clients to perform versus the number that staff members will perform. This, of course, affects price, but it also affects the nature of a trip. Setting up and taking down camp every day is a lot of work, but some clients consider the chore an important element of camping and want to participate. Likewise, rowing a boat is a lot of work that some clients want to do but others do not. Hiking outfitters sometimes vary the rigor of each day's journey and the distance they expect to cover. With some, hikers need to move along at a brisk pace, whereas others allow a more leisurely pace. Choices these vendors make characterize the service they offer and make theirs different from that of their competitors. Providing this information on the organization's website helps distinguish the organization and its products from others.

Video games are sometimes marketed as being designed by a specific designer who has developed a reputation for certain gaming features. These games come with the expectation of a specific style and quality level associated with the designer. Developing a signature character for your experiences can help you capture a specific and unique market niche. Customers should easily be able to articulate the unique nature of the experiences you provide. If they cannot identify the signature character of your experiences, you still have more work to do.

Customizing

We discussed earlier that individuals will have varying reactions to the experiences you create. And these alternate interpretations provide for customizing an event for individuals. But the designer can also intentionally build in touchpoint templates that allow for individual interpretation and action; that is, they can build more affordance into an experience. Bob was once involved in operating a children's summer craft program.

One of the activities was painting plaster cast figurines. Initially, the staff provided children with an example of one already painted. Yes, almost every child tried to duplicate the staff-provided example.

In response, the program organizers identified two options: provide more examples (i.e., more choices) or none at all. So, the staff stopped providing an example and let children come up with their own ideas. This decision increased the activity's affordance—without an example, the children had more interactive possibilities and could experiment with various options to discover their own unique customization. No examples = no preordained choices = nondirective, self-discovery options for participants. Now, left with their choices, some children tried to paint the figures to reflect reality, others painted them abstractly; some used bright, fundamental colors usually used in cartoons, and others just created a mess. But what they did was their choice.

Creating customization sometimes interferes with efficiency and requires more work. But people often want things their way. Another example of customization is staging an organized trip. It's always a risk for the trip leader to release participants to do some things on their own: to give them some freedom to go into shops that interest them, to eat at a restaurant of their liking, to spend more time viewing one piece of art over another, and so on. Although keeping participants herded in a single group led by the trip leader, who is therefore accompanying participants, is the most efficient and sure way of keeping everyone accounted for, this arrangement is often the least satisfying for the participants.

In other experiences, creating customization has become easier and less costly. Computers are so robust today that anything that is computerized can be provided with multiple options with little additional investment. Online shopping experiences are routine and offer countless options for almost any product. You need go no farther than the keyboard of your computer to get access to product inventories that can't possibly be carried in one location by a retail brick-and-mortar store. The most engaging shopping programs are written to make the experience one of discovery, and often the choices offered are sequenced to help consumers build the product they want. Some of the best programs are educational as well and provide excellent content.[13]

Customizing, which allows individual choice, is generally preferred to providing no choice at all. Customization is sometimes more

expensive than noncustomized experiences, however, so the experience designer needs to evaluate the obvious trade-off. B. Joseph Pine II has written extensively on what he calls "mass customization" and discusses the difference between offering variety versus providing actual choice. If you are interested in learning more about this topic, we recommend that you consult his writings.[14] Some caution regarding customizing should also be given, because as Barry Schwartz notes in his best-selling book *The Paradox of Choice*, when it comes to making decisions, more is not always better.[15] In fact, our brains struggle to make decisions when presented with too many options, so use your customization strategies wisely.

Empathy

Empathy is important for designing experiences,[16] as well as for delivering experiences.[17] Showing empathy and understanding a patron's dilemma is a good first response to most problems or situations. This can be done to excess, however, and in some retail outlets it is. For example, employees in one nutrition store that Bob frequents always seem to have the same problem he has, and they can immediately identify a product that solved the problem for them. Remarkable! Empathy works only when it's sincere.

Putting excesses aside, showing sympathy for a customer's plight is always a good way to begin rectifying a situation. When there is a problem with an incorrect charge, for example, a staff member's simple comment, "That is irritating, isn't it? Let's have a look," starts the process on the customer's side. There was no admission of an error, but the possibility that one occurred still exists as the conversation moves forward. Training front-stage staff to respond with this type of general demeanor will ensure that they show customers empathy and understanding.

It's also a good strategy early in a conversation to learn what remedy a patron has in mind. Finding out the end game from the customer's standpoint is very helpful in strategizing the course of the conversation. Doing this immediately gives employees clues about whether they can resolve the concern, whether the expected outcome is realistic and possible, and how to go about concluding the situation. Sometimes customers' initial expectations are unrealistic, and the conversational strategy needs to immediately focus on possible

realistic resolutions. There are also occasions when issues won't come to a satisfactory conclusion and it's best to stop spending time on them as soon as possible.

Experience Deepening

Deep experiences are ones where the anticipation, participation, and reflection phases have been intentionally designed to create harmony across the entire experience. Collectively, a deep experience includes the sociopsychological space occupied by the entire experience. Although all three phases are important, there is a tendency to focus on staging the participation phase while giving less attention to the anticipation and reflection phases. To review a bit from previous chapters, recall that anticipation begins at the first touchpoint of the experience journey map. This could include an advertisement, a word-of-mouth exchange with a previous participant, or texted information from a former participant. These initial contacts are important touchpoints for building expectations about the experience. Experience designers need to take care at this point to make sure they are practicing truth in advertising. Meeting expectations leads to participant satisfaction. Yes, you want to promote your experience, but you must be able to deliver on the expectations you create; otherwise, you will have disappointed and dissatisfied participants.

Designing the participation phase has received adequate treatment elsewhere in the book, so we won't spend more time here on this phase. Actually staging an experience, and thereby implementing the participation phase, is also time consuming; it is the phase where the most time is usually spent. But this occurs after design. Reflection is also an important phase that frequently receives little design attention. Pay close attention to endings; they are the point of separation from your experience. Chip Heath and Dan Heath note that endings are more accurately thought of as transitions from one experience to the next and are excellent opportunities to build intentional peaks.[18] Departing interactions will be the last contact participants have with the experience you have designed, and these interactions are likely to influence the resultant memories they take away. Individuals frequently commiserate or jointly reflect on the experience with others who shared the experience. Texting and other social media are heavily used in this process, and you are well advised to facilitate these

exchanges so that you are aware of the narrative. Often during this process, participants re-create the narrative of the experience and its meaning to them.

Recalling an experience is enhanced when there are objects that cue recall and innumerable artifacts are available as cues. Texted enquiries from you are but one triggering device to facilitate recall. Photographs and videos of the experience are well-known and common cues. Formal acknowledgments, such as certificates, or other acknowledgments specific to an experience are useful. Tee shirts and other physical objects associated with the experience may be included in the purchase price to promote recall. Sometimes recalling an experience involves people, not just objects—for example, follow-up reunions and the like reunite cohorts from the experience.

An experience design will likely pay great attention to the participation phase, but we remind designers that the anticipation and reflection phases can be used effectively to enhance an experience and increase the likelihood of a positive memory.

Memorializing

We briefly touched on memorializing in the previous section. Building in touchpoints intended to help cue lasting memories is always a challenge. Many experience designers try to create a "wow" to provide participants with a unique memory. The problem with this approach is that it requires designers to come up with new and bigger "wows" for repeat participants. That's not to say you shouldn't design for "wow" moments, just make sure the direction they are taking you is possible and sustainable in subsequent operations of the experience.

Photographs and videos of unique moments in experiences create cues for lasting memories as well as "brag points" to share with friends and family. Placing them on YouTube and other accessible web-based platforms provides greater exposure. Given the plethora of souvenirs available for purchase at most events and experiences, photographs and videos are becoming some of the few unique and authentic souvenirs that can be obtained from an experience. Event organizers often expend great effort to provide participants with a unique photo, preferably one with just the participant and important physical elements of the experience. Indeed, on-location photography has become a major revenue stream for many enterprises. Participants are often allowed

to take their own photographs, but in many cases the best angle or spot for a photo is reserved for the commercial photographer, who provides the photo for a fee.

It's important that experience designers know the significant touchpoints in an experience and enhance the memorability of these with appropriate theater or decorum that is specified in the touchpoint template. Let's look again at university commencement exercises. These are usually attended by the family and loved ones of the students who are graduating, as well as a contingent of people required to be there, including faculty and administrators. These ceremonies include much pomp and circumstance, but the single touchpoint most important to many attendees is hearing the name of their student read aloud and seeing their student handed a diploma by a university official. With large numbers of students, completing this exercise becomes more and more of a challenge. Yet, commencement is so important that most universities find some way to accomplish this, either in the main ceremony or in break-out ceremonies organized by individual colleges or some other unit. These ceremonies involve great theater, which is partly created with the colorful regalia faculty members wear. Most other individuals in gown-wearing professions, like judges and clergy, routinely wear their robes when performing their duties. But university faculty members wear their regalia only during commencement exercises, on Founders Day, and on a few other academic occasions during the year. So, great effort and a variety of intentional cues are put forth to make commencement exercises memorable.

Specific theater characterizes other cultural celebrations and rites of passage. Christian baptism, for example, consists of pouring water over a person's forehead or immersing the person in water and anointing him or her with oils, along with saying special prayers. This occasion is usually attended by all close relatives, further signifying the baptism's importance. This ceremony and the accompanying artifacts are used rarely, and thus their use is memorable. Bar mitzvahs and bat mitzvahs are also once-in-a-lifetime rites of passage and initiation ceremonies for young boys and girls in the Jewish faith. Quinceañera is the Hispanic tradition of celebrating a young girl's coming-of-age on her fifteenth birthday that includes religious and cultural rites of passage guiding her from childhood to maturity. Specific cultural or religious microexperiences make each of these occasions memorable.

Chip and Dan Heath highlight four techniques that can be used to memorialize microexperiences or, in other words, transform them from ordinary touchpoints into extraordinary ones:[19]

- *Elevation:* Use surprise and sensory stimuli to make a touchpoint uniquely standout. We'll talk more about sensitizing in the next section as a way to elevate experiences.
- *Insight:* Design opportunities for participants to learn something new about themselves or the world around them. Such touchpoints are designed paradigm shifts or, as we labeled them in chapter 3, transformational experiences.
- *Pride*: Facilitate experiences where participants are able to showcase their best selves. Races, employee recognition events, and service opportunities are all examples of pride-infused experiences.
- *Connection*: Recognize that experiences that help build and strengthen social bonds with others can often be the most powerful type of experiences. This becomes obvious when you reflect on how you cherish memories from experiences where relationships were initiated and or strengthened (e.g., first dates, family reunions, summer camps).

Chip and Dan's book is an excellent read, and we highly recommend that you have a copy in your professional library. It provides many excellent examples about transforming the ordinary or unexpected into what they call "defining moments."

Sensitizing

The importance of sensitizing (i.e., designing to delight and surprise the senses) cannot be overstated. As you design and stage experiences, you should be continuously evaluating the contribution or distraction of each sensory perspective: sight, sound, smell, touch, and taste. Is the lighting appropriate? What does the experience sound like, smell like, feel like, and taste like? Different senses will be salient depending on the experience, but don't overlook any of them, because sensitizing can make or break your experience. You want the sensory cues to align with and complement the overall intended experience. We dealt with this topic in chapter 4 while discussing the role of place in the experiencescape, so feel free to review that section for more insights on sensitizing.

Theming

The importance and power of theming was a major topic in Pine and Gilmore's *The Experience Economy.*[20] We usually do a great job developing theme in familiar events with established theme elements like Christmas, Hanukkah, birthdays, and the Fourth of July. A theme is a recognizable or dominant overarching concept that gives harmony to an experience. We know that hearts, the color red, lace, candy, flowers, and the cupid icon all call out and reinforce a Valentine theme. However, we often do not fully establish and develop a theme for other, less well-known or everyday events. Doing so usually enhances them.

Theming an experience can be as elaborate as the budget allows the designer to achieve. Wedding planners know this and have a large assortment of themed items that can be sold to couples who are being married. Most of the items are themed by personalizing them with the couple's names and wedding date imprinted on them. But today many couples go beyond these stock items. Theming is so important that many couples work with their wedding planner to develop a personal theme, often selecting a theme unique to the couple, something known to their friends, family, and guests. Some examples: honey from the couple's family honey operation, or personalized cozies for beer drinking at a cowboy-themed wedding. Other examples speak to the couple's beliefs or personal projects, such as wildflower seeds from couples committed to natural habitats.[21]

One challenge with theming is investing resources wisely. Theming should reinforce the intended result of the experience in a tasteful and supportive manner. But theming can be done to excess and thereby detract from the experience. Another challenge is to eliminate anything contrary to the theme of an experience; this can be a problem when an organizer rents a venue usually used for a different purpose. For example, universities often use their basketball court or sports arena for commencement exercises. There are usually many visual indicators that this is a sports venue, and eliminating or covering them may be necessary to create an atmosphere suitable for commencement. Bob, who has attended many commencement exercises, has noticed that when they are conducted in a sports venue, people tend to yell out when their student is announced. In contrast, when exercises are held in a theater or auditorium, there is much less of this loud behavior.

Lack of theming can detract from experiences. A good example of this is apparent in many small-town festivals. Although the festivals all have a titular theme, the attending food vendors and many of the arts, crafts, and merchandise vendors travel from festival to festival. They bring their same booth to each of the festivals and sell the same merchandise, thereby creating a boring sameness to these events. Sameness equals low value when uniqueness is the key to a memorable experience. In contrast, most Renaissance festivals are held in more permanent facilities, the food booths are themed, and there is an attempt to provide some uniqueness and theming to the food itself. The retail items that are sold are unique and on theme. In these cases, the food and retail items contribute to theme and thus make a big difference in the experience. All the staff members at Renaissance festivals are costumed on theme. Many spectators who attend these events regularly also wear themed costumes, in this way adding to the authentic, participatory feel of the experience.

As companies increasingly recognize the powerful role experiences can play in connecting customers to brands, the field of experiential marketing has grown dramatically over the last few years. Many corporations feature their brand logo and slogan at events they sponsor and sometimes use both as the basis of a theme. These companies carefully choose events and other experiences to sponsor, looking for those that are truly associated with their product or the customers of their product.

In some of his research Mat has seen theming both positively and negatively affect companies' efforts to provide their employees valued nonwork experiences at their place of work (e.g., company parties, workout facilities, game rooms). He conducted interviews with employees at a software company that held sporting tournaments (e.g., sand volleyball, frisbee football, softball) every Friday during the summer. He found that this was great for those employees who liked sports, but the company employed many software engineers, and there was some grumbling from the employees who preferred video games over sports. In contrast to this example, Mat also interviewed employees at an outdoor gear company that encouraged employees to spend 10 percent of their work week "in the wild." Employees really enjoyed this policy because many of them had chosen to work in this industry because they loved outdoor recreation. The point is that you should make sure the theme you choose fits your brand and the preferences of the employees.

A Cautionary Tale

As a final contemporary example of why correct sequencing of the experience design process is so important, consider the case of the Fyre Festival.[22] Starting in 2016, event organizers and a supportive pool of social-media influencers began promoting Fyre Festival as a two-week luxury music festival on the island of Great Exuma in the Bahamas. The festival was billed as the event of the year, and VIP ticket packages priced at over $100,000 were available. The marketing lead-up to the event painted an amazing picture of big-name performers, beautiful people in luxury island accommodations, and five-star dining experiences. This was the frosting. Unfortunately, the cake was horrible.

When attendees, many of whom had paid thousands of dollars to attend, began to arrive on Great Exuma toward the end of April 2017, they were surprised to encounter what looked more like a refugee camp than a luxury music festival. Patrons who had been promised luxury glamping accommodations were offered what looked like disaster-relief tents. The food provided consisted of bread, cheese, and lettuce in Styrofoam containers. To top it off, there was not enough water and no electricity for most attendees. What was supposed to have been a two-week festival was shut down after the first day, leaving people who had already landed on Great Exuma stranded and those still trying to get to the island stuck in mainland airports. Disgruntled attendees who felt they had been tricked took to social media and unleashed a firestorm of negative backlash toward the event's organizers. The event's founder, Billy McFarland, has pled guilty to multiple wire fraud charges, and the entire Fyre Festival debacle has been turned into a Hulu documentary series.[23] Not only can jumping immediately to final enhancements ruin an experience, it can also significantly damage careers and brands.

Summary: The Icing on the Cake

We've said from the beginning of this book that experience design is a complex endeavor. It takes time and intentional concentrated effort to work through the process of experience design thinking, but it's

worth it. Your efforts will result in experiences that are much more likely to delight end users and produce targeted results. The areas for experience enhancement discussed in this chapter will provide you with some great ways to embellish your experiences. There are, of course, many more than we can cover here; but we hope this chapter has helped prime your creative pump to come up with even more enhancements. Think of them as additional tools in your toolbox. You won't use them for every experience design project, but at least you'll be aware of the options at your disposal.

There are a lot of steps and pieces to consider when designing experiences, and in this chapter, we've added even more things to think about. Remember, though, not all the factors introduced in this chapter need to be applied in every experience. Given that we started this chapter with a baking analogy, let's use another comparison to wrap things up. Most baking recipes follow a similar pattern. You mix the wet ingredients and dry ingredients separately, then you combine them, and finally you bake whatever it is you're making. While the process remains the same across most recipes, what differentiates the end products is the unique combination of ingredients called for in each recipe. This is how you can use the same process and end up with brownies one time and peanut-butter cookies the next.

Now consider the experience design processes introduced in part 2 of this book. This is the basic process we recommend that you follow when designing experiences. What makes each experience unique is not the process; it's the ingredients, which in the case of experiences are the unique combination of experiencescape elements and the technical and artistic factors discussed in this chapter. Just as master chefs will not try to use every ingredient at their disposal when making a dish, so too will master experience designers selectively choose the appropriate combination of elements and factors to create the perfect experience.

You've almost made it to the end of our book—one more chapter to go. We've made the point from the beginning of the book that all organizations are in the business of staging experiences whether they recognize it or not. This means the experience design process should be used by all organizations. We also believe the experience design process can be used to think innovatively about other areas of business, including product development and corporate strategy. We'll address both areas in the next chapter.

CHAPTER TEN

Using Experience Design in Product Development and Corporate Strategy

THE TECHNIQUES WE have taught you throughout previous chapters work in any experience design situation. In this chapter we'll look specifically at product development and corporate strategy. We believe that product development that is focused on the use of a product in an experience is one of the more difficult design problems. In this chapter we're going to demonstrate how the experience design process described in this book can be used to embed products in experience journeys to enhance the product development process. For our example we're going to design an experience around a digital golfers' tool called Golf Buddy©.

Golf Buddy is a chip-based electronic device that uses a GPS to determine the distance a golf ball lies from the hole in the targeted green. This helps golfers select the correct club for a shot, as each club will hit the ball a different distance. Each golfer hits each club a little differently, but most golfers know how far they can hit a ball with each specific club. Often the unknown variable is the distance the ball must be hit in a given situation. Without some type of assistive device, the golfer must estimate the distance. Most courses have colored-marker

poles at the 100- and 150-foot distances from the green. But rarely is your ball next to one of these poles.

So, distance remains a mystery. Some golfers can remember distances once they have played a course; most cannot. Professional golfers and their caddies scout courses in advance of competitive play, and the caddies take extensive notes about distances, obstacles, slope, and other factors relevant to each hole on a specific course. But most everyday golfers could use help with some of these contingencies, especially distance.

Golf Buddy is a simple and reasonably priced product that enhances the everyday golfer's experience of playing golf. The device is available in different configurations, including a fob that can be clipped to a belt loop or your golf bag as well as a wristwatch type of setup for wearing the device on an arm. When in use, the device shows the distance remaining to a specific hole and also offers an alternate program that enables players to determine the distance of the shot they just completed. This latter feature helps golfers make a more accurate club selection by helping them learn how far they can hit with each club. Distances reported are accurate, and the device is easy to use. Golfers can use it unobtrusively while playing the game. It works at almost every golf course in the United States, and golfers can access and download international courses from the Golf Buddy website.

The main skills in golf are, of course, hitting a shot the correct distance and in the right direction. Golf Buddy does not substitute or change either of these skills—golfers must still acquire and exhibit these skills. The program does remove the uncertainty about the length of the next shot. Thus, Golf Buddy provides important information that enhances the golfing experience, and a player's interactive experience with the device is usually positive.

The Golf Buddy Experience Journey

The Golf Buddy accompanies a golfer during a round of golf. This is a known, intentional, and routine experience journey. Each of the eighteen episodes of a round of golf follows the same scenario. The golfer must tee off, take a varying number of shots from the fairway toward the green, perhaps execute a chip or approach shot, and finally putt. The intention is, of course, to take as few shots as possible to put the ball in the cup on each tee. But the game is not monotonous;

every one of the eighteen holes of a golf course and each golf course itself is designed differently. To be a true buddy, Golf Buddy will need to help the golfer take fewer shots. So, the intention of Golf Buddy is to help golfers reduce the number of strokes they take during a round and thus improve their score. To be marketable, the program will need to be in a price point with other golf accessories. What follows are the details of the experience journey, its touchpoints and transitions.

Touchpoints and Transitions of the Golf Buddy Experience

The specifics of each touchpoint in an experience journey is planned and represented in the graphs shown in figures 10.1 through 10.6. Following are our thoughts about how these designs would be planned, graphed, and accomplished.

Touchpoint Template #1—The Macroexperience of Playing Golf with Golf Buddy

You will notice in this touchpoint that the desired reaction from using the product is that "Golf Buddy was easy to use and improved my game." The experiencescape elements in this experience include the golfer (participant), a golf course, Golf Buddy, golf balls, golf clubs, and playing partners. The two critical designed interactions are the golfer's ability to easily operate Golf Buddy and the device's provision of accurate, reliable information. Backstage contributors include computer programmers who will make Golf Buddy's use unobtrusive but accurate and a manufacturer who can make a reliable, attractive product. The co-creation intended is that the golfer who is interacting with Golf Buddy will play a better round of golf. The primary desired technical enhancement is reliable operation. The two primary artistic factors include good product design and good graphic display. So, a product that is reliable, accurate, and easy to use while golfing is the sum of the experience desired.

Touchpoint Template #2—Meeting Your Golf Buddy

This touchpoint is intended to be a mindful experience because it mostly involves learning with an additional intention to excite the

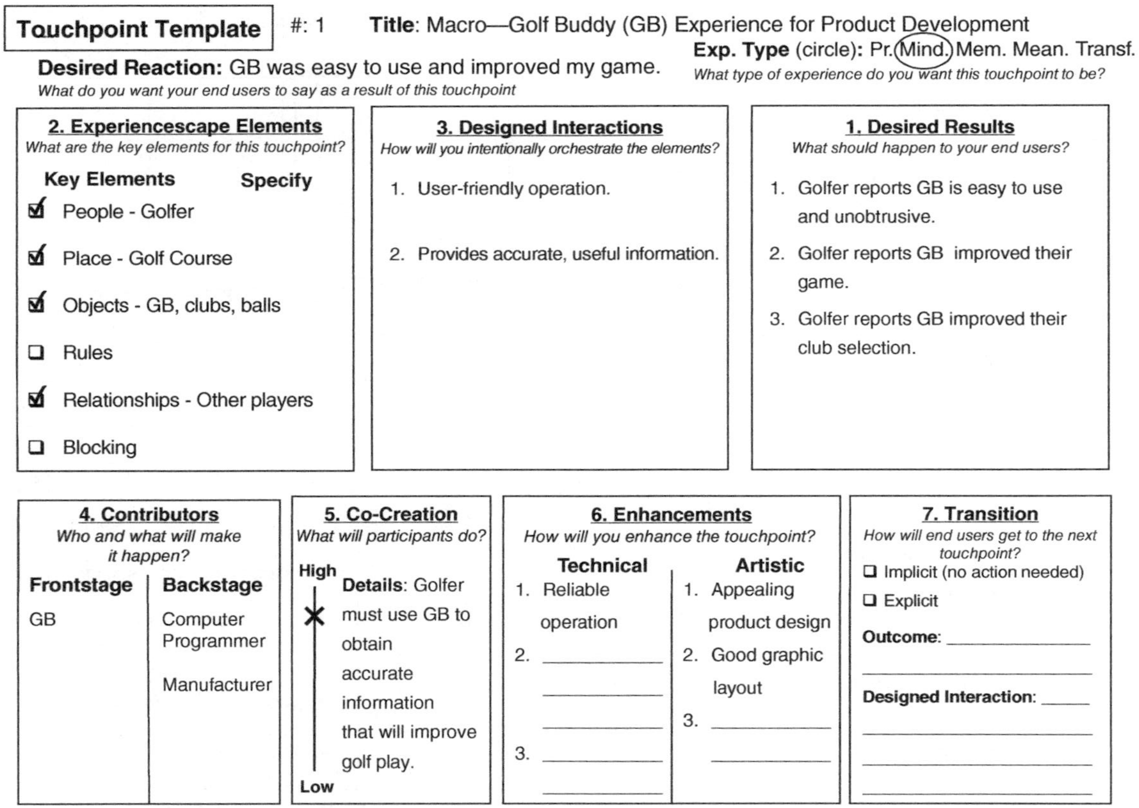

Touchpoint Template #: 1 **Title**: Macro—Golf Buddy (GB) Experience for Product Development

Exp. Type (circle)**:** Pr. (Mind.) Mem. Mean. Transf.
What type of experience do you want this touchpoint to be?

Desired Reaction: GB was easy to use and improved my game.
What do you want your end users to say as a result of this touchpoint

2. Experiencescape Elements
What are the key elements for this touchpoint?

Key Elements **Specify**

- ☑ People - Golfer
- ☑ Place - Golf Course
- ☑ Objects - GB, clubs, balls
- ☐ Rules
- ☑ Relationships - Other players
- ☐ Blocking

3. Designed Interactions
How will you intentionally orchestrate the elements?

1. User-friendly operation.
2. Provides accurate, useful information.

1. Desired Results
What should happen to your end users?

1. Golfer reports GB is easy to use and unobtrusive.
2. Golfer reports GB improved their game.
3. Golfer reports GB improved their club selection.

4. Contributors
Who and what will make it happen?

Frontstage	Backstage
GB	Computer Programmer
	Manufacturer

5. Co-Creation
What will participants do?

High – X – Low

Details: Golfer must use GB to obtain accurate information that will improve golf play.

6. Enhancements
How will you enhance the touchpoint?

Technical	Artistic
1. Reliable operation	1. Appealing product design
2. ______	2. Good graphic layout
3. ______	3. ______

7. Transition
How will end users get to the next touchpoint?

- ☐ Implicit (no action needed)
- ☐ Explicit

Outcome: ______

Designed Interaction: ______

Figure 10.1 Touchpoint template 1.

Touchpoint Template #: 2 **Title**: Meeting Your Golf Buddy (GB) **Exp. Type** (circle): Pr. (Mind.) Mem. Mean. Transf.
What type of experience do you want this touchpoint to be?

Desired Reaction: This was easy to learn. I can't wait to use my GB.
What do you want your end users to say as a result of this touchpoint

2. Experiencescape Elements
What are the key elements for this touchpoint?

Key Elements **Specify**

- ☑ People - Golfer
- ☑ Place - Golf Course
- ☑ Objects - GB, clubs, balls
- ☐ Rules
- ☑ Relationships - Other players
- ☐ Blocking

3. Designed Interactions
How will you intentionally orchestrate the elements?

1. Golfer reads instructions.
2. Golfer interacts with GB.
3. Golfer must charge GB.

1. Desired Results
What should happen to your end users?

1. Golfer reports instructions are easy to read and clear.
2. Golfer reports they understand how to use and is excited to try using GB.
3. Golfer reports charging is easy.

4. Contributors
Who and what will make it happen?

Frontstage	Backstage
GB	

5. Co-Creation
What will participants do?

High

X **Details**: Learning to use is self-taught

Low

6. Enhancements
How will you enhance the touchpoint?

Technical	Artistic
1. Clear instructions	1. Good graphics

7. Transition
How will end users get to the next touchpoint?

- ☐ Implicit (no action needed)
- ☐ Explicit

Outcome: ____________

Designed Interaction: ______

Figure 10.2 Touchpoint template 2.

golfer about playing golf with the Golf Buddy. The desired reactions from touchpoint template 2 are that "this was easy to use" and that the player felt "anticipation to use Golf Buddy." The experiencescape elements are the golfer, the Golf Buddy, and the written instructions accompanying the device. Three interactions need to occur to accomplish the desired reactions: reading the instructions, interacting with the Golf Buddy via the instructions, and charging the Golf Buddy. This touchpoint is, certainly, high on co-creation because the golfer must do the reading to learn how to use the Golf Buddy. A critical enhancement is clear communication. The instructional flyer that comes with the product is simple to read, is only one-page long, and has great graphics. The immediate subliminal message from the flyer is that this is going to be short and easy, and indeed it is.

Touchpoint Template #3—Initiating Play

Upon arriving at the course, the golfer must turn on Golf Buddy. This is accomplished by simply turning on a switch, and the Golf Buddy subsequently announces its progress as it locates satellites and finds the golf course being played. Once this is done, the golfer is directed to move to the first tee. The distance from the golfer's location to the cup is displayed on Golf Buddy at the start of the game. The golfer then proceeds as usual and takes the first shot unless he or she decides to implement touchpoint template 3a, having Golf Buddy track the distance of the shot. Golf Buddy informs play but does not disrupt or change it. The player then proceeds to the ball and implements touchpoint template 3a or touchpoint template 4.

Touchpoint Template #3a—Educational Alternate Experience Journey

Touchpoint template 3a is an alternative touchpoint that occurs if a golfer wants to know how far he or she has hit a shot. By pushing a button before hitting the ball, the player can set up Golf Buddy to report the distance of the shot. Some players like to know the distance of their tee shot and will use this feature once each hole. Others like to know how far they can hit various clubs and will use this feature as their interest dictates. Usually, once a player learns how far he or she hits various clubs, the use for this purpose will wane.

Touchpoint Template #: 3 **Title**: Initiating Play **Exp. Type** (circle): Pr. (Mind. Mem.) Mean. Transf.

What type of experience do you want this touchpoint to be?

Desired Reaction: This is easy. I played a better game.

What do you want your end users to say as a result of this touchpoint

2. Experiencescape Elements

What are the key elements for this touchpoint?

Key Elements	Specify
☑ People	Golfer
☑ Place	Golf Course
☑ Objects	GB, clubs, balls
☐ Rules	
☑ Relationships	Other players
☐ Blocking	

3. Designed Interactions

How will you intentionally orchestrate the elements?

1. Golfer must turn on GB. Everything else is automatic.
2. Golfer is informed that he or she is on hole one and the yardage to the cup.
3. Golfer must play golf (i.e., take their shot).

1. Desired Results

What should happen to your end users?

1. That was easy. I am ready to play.
2. This is great. I know which club to use.
3. Satisfaction with shot and purchase of GB.
4. Some shots will be memorable.

4. Contributors

Who and what will make it happen?

Frontstage	Backstage
	Programmers

5. Co-Creation

What will participants do?

High

Details: Low____

GB–Easy to use

Playing golf—High

Improved because of critical information provided by GB

Low

6. Enhancements

How will you enhance the touchpoint?

Technical	Artistic
1. ________	1. ________
2. ________	2. ________
3. ________	3. ________

7. Transition

How will end users get to the next touchpoint?

☐ Implicit (no action needed)

☒ Explicit

Outcome: Golfer selects continuing with TT 3a or TT 4

Designed Interaction: This is a one choice interaction and the options are explained in TT #3a and TT #4

Figure 10.3 Touchpoint template 3.

Touchpoint Template #: 3a **Title**: Educational Alternate Experience Journey **Exp. Type** (circle): Pr. (Mind) Mem. Mean. Transf.
What type of experience do you want this touchpoint to be?

Desired Reaction: I am learning the distance I hit with my different clubs.
What do you want your end users to say as a result of this touchpoint

2. Experiencescape Elements
What are the key elements for this touchpoint?

Key Elements **Specify**

- ☑ People - Golfer
- ☑ Place - Golf Course
- ☑ Objects - GB, clubs, balls
- ☐ Rules
- ☐ Relationships
- ☐ Blocking

3. Designed Interactions
How will you intentionally orchestrate the elements?

1. Golfer must signal GB to track shot distance by pressing button at starting location and ending location.

1. Desired Results
What should happen to your end users?

1. Golfer learns how far they can hit each specific club.

4. Contributors
Who and what will make it happen?

Frontstage	Backstage

5. Co-Creation
What will participants do?

High ✕ — Low

Details: Takes more Interaction to achieve this learning

6. Enhancements
How will you enhance the touchpoint?

Technical	Artistic
1. ______	1. ______
2. ______	2. ______
3. ______	3. ______

7. Transition
How will end users get to the next touchpoint?

- ☐ Implicit (no action needed)
- ☑ Explicit–Golfer decision

Outcome: Learn shot distances

Designed Interaction: Self Education. Then resume TT #4 - Can continue this iteration throughout game

Figure 10.4 Touchpoint template 3a.

Touchpoint Template #: 4 **Title**: Continuing Play **Exp. Type** (circle): Pr. (Mind. Mem. Mean) Transf.

What type of experience do you want this touchpoint to be?

Desired Reaction: This is really helping me play better golf.

What do you want your end users to say as a result of this touchpoint

2. Experiencescape Elements

What are the key elements for this touchpoint?

Key Elements **Specify**

- ☑ People - Golfer
- ☑ Place - Golf Course
- ☑ Objects - GB, clubs, balls
- ☐ Rules
- ☑ Relationships - Other players
- ☐ Blocking

3. Designed Interactions

How will you intentionally orchestrate the elements?

1. Second shot (next shot) GB displays distance to hole.
2. Better club selection results in better shots and overall play.
3. Other players are impressed and ask their shot distances.

1. Desired Results

What should happen to your end users?

1. Succeeding shots are better—overall golf game is improved.
2. Some shots are memorable and even occasionally meaningful.
3. Friendship bonding and goodwill with other players resulting from providing friends with useful information.

4. Contributors

Who and what will make it happen?

Frontstage | **Backstage**

5. Co-Creation

What will participants do?

High

Low

Details: _____

6. Enhancements

How will you enhance the touchpoint?

Technical	**Artistic**
1. _____	1. _____
2. _____	2. _____
3. _____	3. _____

7. Transition

How will end users get to the next touchpoint?

- ☐ Implicit (no action needed)
- ☑ Explicit

Outcome: Easy, as it occurs automatically through GPS as one moves through the course. TT #4 to TT #3 + #3a to #4 and so on through 18 holes of golf.

Figure 10.5 Touchpoint template 4.

Touchpoint Template #: 5 **Title**: End of Play **Exp. Type** (circle): Pr. (Cons. Mind. Mean.) Transf.

What type of experience do you want this touchpoint to be?

Desired Reaction: Golf Buddy is useful and improved my play.

What do you want your end users to say as a result of this touchpoint

2. Experiencescape Elements

What are the key elements for this touchpoint?

Key Elements	Specify
☑ People	Golfer
☐ Place	
☑ Objects	GB
☐ Rules	
☑ Relationships	Other players
☐ Blocking	

3. Designed Interactions

How will you intentionally orchestrate the elements?

1. Golfer switches off GB.
2. Golfer converses with other players about the game and perhaps the usefulness of GB.

1. Desired Results

What should happen to your end users?

1. Golfer recognizes the how GB positively impacted this round of golf.
2. Golfer anticipates using GB in future rounds of golf.
3. Golfer converses with other players about the round and the usefulness of GB. Depending on the player's score, the round may be memorable or meaningful.

4. Contributors

Who and what will make it happen?

Frontstage	Backstage

5. Co-Creation

What will participants do?

High

Details: ______

Low

6. Enhancements

How will you enhance the touchpoint?

Technical	Artistic
1. ______	1. ______
2. ______	2. ______
3. ______	3. ______

7. Transition

How will end users get to the next touchpoint?

☑ Implicit (no action needed)

☐ Explicit

Outcome: ______

Designed Interaction: ______

Figure 10.6 Touchpoint template 5.

Touchpoint Template #4—Continuing Play

Once the player arrives at the destination of the shot taken, Golf Buddy immediately displays the distance remaining to the hole. This information is updated automatically with the GPS, and the player need do nothing except read the information from the display screen. Also, because hole locations on greens are moved frequently, Golf Buddy displays three locations—front, middle, and back—to increase accuracy. The result intended from the information Golf Buddy provides is an improved golf game, which should result in more memorable and meaningful experiences. A further benefit is that the player's real-life golf buddies appreciate being allowed to use Golf Buddy to calculate their own shot distances.

The continuing transitions, then, are iterating between touchpoint template 3, 3a, and 4 through the entire eighteen holes of golf. If a player does not use the touchpoint template 3a feature, everything is automatic and all the player must do is read the information from the display screen to make certain he or she is using the information about the current location of the hole. This is quickly and easily done when selecting a club from a golf bag. Using the Golf Buddy is seamless and does not interfere with the usual flow of a golf game. Banter between friends, strategizing a shot, setting up for a shot, taking the shot, and so on all proceed as usual.

The continual iteration of touchpoint templates 3, 3a, and 4 through each hole may seem repetitive. But remember, each hole is different. Each has a different distance and par, and each uses various hazards, including water, moguls, and bunkers. Although the Golf Buddy operates the same way each time, each succeeding hole is a different experience because of the unique design of each hole.

Touchpoint Template #5—End of Play

When finished with a round, the golfer must switch off Golf Buddy. If the golfer forgets, the device will turn itself off after a period of inactivity. The reactions intended at this point are reflection about the usefulness of Golf Buddy while playing a round and anticipation of using it in future rounds. The manufacturer, of course, hopes that the reflection is positive, that the golfer sees Golf Buddy as a positive contributor to the game. At this point the golfer transitions back to touchpoint template 2 to recharge the unit.

Summary—The Golf Buddy Experience

Using Golf Buddy is easy and unobtrusive. Whether it improves a player's game is not certain, but it is possible. So, one of Golf Buddy's two intended reactions is assured—it is a product likely to receive a favorable review. Part of its effectiveness is how well it fits into experiencing flow in a game of golf. This objective is to some degree achieved because of the targeted affordance the Golf Buddy was designed to provide.

The GPS and computer-chip technology are robust, and many more features could have been included. For example, stats on how well a player previously played a certain hole and the player's lifetime average for a specific hole could have been built in. A player's average distance per club could have been added as well—all potentially neat features. But the designers chose not to add these extras because they understood how their product was going to be used in the golf experience. Golfers need a buddy, someone or something that cares enough about them and their golf game to make it better, not something that will demand so much attention that it detracts from playing golf and interacting with their real-life golf buddies. So, there is a sweet spot for affordance that must be realized depending on the role a product will play in the experience drama. The product may not be the lead actor, just a supporting one. Do not get this wrong. More features do not always equate to a better product. Understanding the experience in which a product will be used informs these decisions in a way no other perspective can.

Experience Design and Corporate Strategy

Corporations are taking notice of experiences. The notion of experience is increasingly found in their missions, values statements, and strategic plans. More and more organizations are appointing chief experience officers to ensure oversight and coordination of the organization's experience design and delivery efforts.[1] In this section we'll share examples of corporations that have made the delivery of excellent experiences a central pillar of their strategic planning. The following examples represent only a small sample of corporate strategies related to experience, but we hope they provide you with some valuable insights into the ways corporations are focusing on experiences.

Restaurants

Fox Restaurant Concepts is a Phoenix-based company with a growing line of nearly fifty unique restaurant concepts across sixteen states. On its website Fox shares the following organizational belief: "We believe the best stories are shared over food. . . . We create spaces that evoke emotion, because we believe food is all about the experience and being able to connect with those who matter."[2] How does the company deliver a great dining experience? The website further states:

> We challenge ourselves to find ways to make our best ideas even better. Every day. We understand that the only way to guarantee our guests the best experience is to constantly refine and perfect it. So when we create new concepts in our test kitchen, we immerse ourselves in all the little details—from the uniforms to the menus, from the food to the music, from the lighting to the linens, all the way down to the salt and pepper shakers—and rework things until they all fit together perfectly.[3]

We hope reading this statement made you think about artistic factors and elements of the experiencescape. Notice how the company works to make the various elements of a new experience speak together in harmony.[4] Fox has applied sound experience design principles to create its restaurant experience. You now have the tools you need to accomplish focused, intentional design in a variety of endeavors. The process you've learned in this book is easily generalizable.

Brinker International, a casual dining restaurant company with more than sixteen hundred restaurants in a variety of countries, welcomes more than one million guests a day into the company's Chili's and Maggiano's restaurants. In its "Making People Feel Special" commitment on the company website, Brinker International states, "We're driven by integrity, teamwork and passion—plus an unwavering commitment for every Guest to have an exceptional dining experience when visiting our brands."[5] How does the company ensure this? Chief Executive Officer and President Wyman T. Roberts, in Brinker's 2016 Annual Report, shared his executive-level thinking about the dining experiences his company hopes to provide: "We are leveraging the heritage of the Chili's brand and increasing media weight to tell the story

of investments in culinary innovation and a dining experience like no place else."[6]

Experience innovations currently being implemented in Brinker International's Maggiano's Little Italy brand include responding to two specific dining experience needs desired by the clientele: carryout and delivery. In some cases, Brinker has built new restaurants with a smaller footprint because there is no need to provide a dining area for carryout and delivery orders. The company is also identifying specific experiences to co-create with customers, including offering cooking classes, wine education classes, and murder mystery events. It wants Maggiano's to be the location of choice for families and friends who are celebrating a memorable event; at the same time, it wants to provide companies with unique engagement opportunities for their employees.[7] Each of these business strategies is focused on specific customer experiences that have been identified as actionable and marketable.

Retail and Consumer Goods

In January 2018 Amazon opened its first Amazon Go grocery store in Seattle, and now Amazon has plans to open two additional stores in San Francisco and Seattle.[8] These stores are Amazon's attempt to completely redesign the grocery story experience by removing the checkout line. Thanks to cameras and shelf sensors, all items placed into shopper's bags are tracked and recorded. When individuals are done shopping, all they have to do is walk out and they are automatically charged for the items in their bags. Amazon's broader strategy to disrupt the grocery industry involves the online sale of groceries and the company's acquisition of Whole Foods, but all this points to a strategic effort to redesign the experience of buying groceries.

Hasbro, the largest toy manufacturer in the world, shares the following corporate goal on its website: "Hasbro is a global play and entertainment company committed to *Creating the World's Best Play Experiences*."[9] The toy company owns some of the most iconic game brands that you have likely played and enjoyed with friends and family. These include Monopoly©, Scrabble©, and Chutes and Ladders©. These games remain popular because they have great affordance; that

is, they provide opportunities for a variety of different experience for players within the context created by the rules of the various games. Hasbro has recently moved to patent the smell of playdough.[10] This also shows that Hasbro understands the important role sensory elements play in experiences, a topic discussed in chapters 4 and 9.

Hospitality and Tourism

You should have known we couldn't help adding a Disney example to this section. In 2017 Disney announced plans for a *Star Wars*–themed hotel to open at Walt Disney World. In 2018 Disney provided more details about this project, describing the hotel as

> a first-of-its-kind resort will combine luxury with complete immersion into an authentic *Star Wars* story. . . . At the resort, guests immediately become active citizens of the galaxy and can dress up in the proper attire. . . . The opportunity for immersion at this resort will also stand out among all Disney resorts around the globe, as it will be seamlessly connected to *Star Wars*: Galaxy's Edge at Disney's Hollywood Studios, allowing guests a total *Star Wars* experience.[11]

We're excited to see how this new experience is received by the public. Remember how we emphasized the importance of storytelling in experience design in chapter 8? The *Star Wars* hotel is a bold example of leveraging the power of a well-known story to design immersive, co-created experiences.

Holland America Line doubles down on experiences in its mission statement: "Through excellence, we create once-in-a-lifetime experiences, every time."[12] Cruises are an expensive and relatively long engagement. For many people cruising is a one-off experience. Although Holland America Line cruises offer many different itineraries, they include a number of themed programs and services that provide uniformity for each sailing. Examples include an evening at Le Cirque and a Culinary Arts Center on each ship, along with other programs that make each Holland America Line sailing similar. Through these consistent programs, a corporate brand is developed and maintained.

Home Building

Lennar, one of the nation's premier "home builders," has been building homes since 1954. The company builds in nineteen states in forty markets. A home is the single most expensive item most people ever buy. Building and purchasing a home is a fairly complicated task that involves designers, builders, financers, title closers, insurance agents, and so on. At its "my Lennar" website, the company provides an online resource "to begin a simplified home purchase and ownership experience."[13] Lennar then provides access to interactive technology of web-based suppliers and vendors of all that is needed to select, build, and purchase a home.

Technology

After completing his MBA, in 2012, Ben Rabner started working full time for Adobe as a web and content strategist for Adobe Experience Cloud. As he observed the effectiveness, or lack thereof, of traditional lead-generation techniques like cocktail parties and steak dinners for executives, he began to sense an opportunity to redesign how Adobe went about building relationships with potential clients. Given his background in competitive road cycling and a rising interest among corporate executives in the sport, Rabner lighted on the idea of staging curated road rides for executives at large international technology conferences.

Ben Rabner saw these curated road rides as an opportunity for Adobe to provide corporate executives a chance to do something they love while traveling and still accomplishing business objectives. This empathetic insight started him on a path from creating a few rides a year as a side project while managing the content team, to his 2015 appointment to his current position as head of experiential marketing for Adobe. The success of his efforts was largely driven by measuring their effect on business and the incredible response from executives about the cycling events and how they helped Adobe build relationships that ultimately influenced revenue and relationships. Adobe continues to expand experiences to include hiking, culinary arts, and photography for executives. The trend of using cycling and other recreational experiences to build corporate relationships is being rapidly adopted across a variety of industries globally.[14]

Summary—The Experience Economy Requires Experience Design

We have taken a long journey into experience design. We have demonstrated in this chapter how experience design concepts and techniques may be used to develop a product by contextualizing it in the experience it will facilitate. Envisioning a product's use in an experience and then actually developing the product with this experiential use in mind is one of the more complicated experience design problems. Using the realities and interactions of an actual experience as one of the design criteria seems intimidating. In reality, constant focus on use as the sideboards of a design problem often enables insightful solutions that would otherwise be inaccessible. We hope this demonstration helps you become a better experience designer.

Corporations from all industries are paying more attention to experiences. Chief experience officers are being hired to ensure that good experiences are delivered consistently across their organizations. Experience and experience outcomes are appearing as strategic initiatives as well as specific outcomes in corporate plans. Yes, experience matters to participants, and many companies are focusing their strategic efforts on providing not just products and services but also outstanding experiences. It is clear that companies that deliver great experiences thrive and those that don't die.

Conclusion

Closing Thoughts

THANKS FOR GOING on this journey with us. We wrote this book to introduce you to approaches and tools that will allow you to practice experience design more effectively and systematically. We hope that we've accomplished this goal. Reading about and engaging in experience design are two different things. You may already be actively involved in experience design, or this book may be your first exposure to the topic. Either way, we encourage you to use the tools we have discussed as you design experiences.

We're both educators, so we can't help but give you a homework assignment as you finish this book. Consider it your personal experience design professional-development project—a type of self-certification in experience design. Here's what we'd like you to do:

1. Pick an experience, be it personal or professional, that you would like to design or redesign.
2. Identify some actual or potential end users (you could even be the end user, depending on what type of experience you're designing) and talk to them, observe them, and develop some empathy for them. Try to understand the experience you're designing or redesigning from their perspective and create their persona(s).
3. Based on what you find out, follow the steps outlined in chapter 5 to develop a point-of-view statement, and then start ideating.
4. Create an experience map prototype based on the results of your ideation, using the guidelines in chapter 6. Consider shaping your experience map with an underlying narrative or heroic journey, as we discussed in chapter 8.

5. After you complete the experience map, make sure to test it out on an end user. Have the person vicariously experience (i.e., visualize) your prototype and provide feedback. Revise your experience map based on the feedback received. Continue revising and testing as necessary.
6. Once you've got the experience map sufficiently polished, use the touchpoint template introduced in chapter 7 to build each touchpoint of your mapped experience.
7. The result of these efforts will be an experience map and a compilation of touchpoint templates that will serve as the blueprints for staging the experience.

Once you've completed this process, do it again for another experience. Over time, the process will become less of a step-by-step approach and more of an ingrained philosophy and operational protocol for designing experiences. Although we recommend that when you first start designing experiences, you follow these outlined steps exactly as shown, keep in mind that as your expertise develops over time, you will tweak and integrate these approaches and tools to best fit your own style and the experience design opportunities you encounter.

The process of designing and then staging experiences can be extremely fulfilling. Seeing an experience progress from a mental concept to a tangible encounter for your end user is rewarding. Experience design also takes courage, because when you hand over the experience you've designed to end users, you may have created something that never existed before and you're never quite sure how they will respond. Will they like it? Will they want to try it again? Such thoughts must have been going through Walt Disney's mind on the opening day of Disneyland. When the experience design works, it's exhilarating. Sharon Baird, one of the original Mouseketeers, fondly remembers the emotional significance that moment held for Walt:

> On the opening day of Disneyland, we [Mouseketeers] were in Walt Disney's private apartment above the Main Street Fire Station when the gates of the park opened for the first time. I was standing next to him at the window, watching the guests come pouring through the gates. When I looked up at him, he had his hands behind his back, a grin from ear to ear, I could see a lump in his throat and a tear streaming down his cheek. He had realized his dream.[1]

Although you most likely won't design and build the world's most iconic theme park, you will feel a similar sense of fulfillment from delivering well-designed experiences to people who value them enough to remember them and their impact. This, more than any other reason, is why we wrote this book. We want you to succeed in designing experiences. The information and tools included in this book will give you confidence to design experiences. Finally, we want you to feel the sense of fulfillment that comes from seeing others be positively affected by the experiences you've designed for them. Good luck!

J. Robert Rossman (Bob),
Phoenix, AZ
Mathew D. Duerden (Mat),
Provo, UT

Notes

1. Exploring Experiences and Experience Design

1. NICE Satmetrix, "U.S. Consumer 2018 Net Promoter Benchmarks at a Glance," *NICE Satmetrix*, 2018, http://info.nice.com/rs/338-EJP-431/images/NICE-Satmetrix-infographic-2018-b2c-nps-benchmarks-050418.pdf.

2. Frederick Reichheld, "The One Number You Need to Grow," *Harvard Business Review* (December 2003), https://hbr.org/2003/12/the-one-number-you-need-to-grow.

3. The NPS scale is 1–10. However, in computing a final score, these raw scores are converted to percentages, resulting in a double-digit final score. NPS is widely used throughout numerous organizations to obtain a read on customer and employee brand loyalty. Nevertheless, the reader is cautioned that NPS is an attention-directing device, not a diagnostic one. A low score for your industry informs you that something is not going right. Additional analysis is necessary to figure out what is malfunctioning. For more information on using NPS, we recommend Frederick Reichheld and Rob Markey, *The Ultimate Question 2.0* (Boston: Harvard Business Review Press, 2011).

4. B. Joseph Pine II and James H. Gilmore, *The Experience Economy: Work Is Theatre and Every Business a Stage* (Boston: Harvard Business School Press, 1999).

5. B. Joseph Pine II and James H. Gilmore, *The Experience Economy*, updated ed. (Boston: Harvard Business Review Press, 2011).

6. Clay Shirky, *Cognitive Surplus: Creativity and Generosity in a Connected Age* (New York: Penguin, 2010), 21.

7. Gary Ellis, Keynote Address, Experience Industry Management Conference, Brigham Young University, Provo, UT, March 21–22, 2013.

8. Paul Ratner, "Want Happiness? Buy Experiences, Not Things, Says a Cornell Psychologist," *Big Think*, July 22, 2016, http://bigthink.com/paul-ratner/want-happiness-buy-experiences-not-more-stuff; Elizabeth Dunn and Michael Norton, *Happy Money: The Science of Happier Spending* (New York: Simon & Schuster, 2014).

9. Erik Qualman, *Socialnomics: How Social Media Transforms the Way We Live and Do Business*, 2nd ed. (Hoboken, NJ: Wiley, 2012); David Meerman Scott, *The New Rules of Marketing and PR* (Hoboken, NJ: Wiley, 2017), 65.

10. Patricia Laya, "Nightmare: 7 Customer Service Blunders That Went Viral," *Business Insider*, June 17, 2011, http://www.businessinsider.com/7-very-public-lessons-in-customer-service-2011-6.

11. Josh Bersin, Jason Flynn, Art Mazor, and Veronica Melian, "Rewriting the Rules for the Digital Age," Deloitte Insights, *2017 Global Human Capital Trends*, February 28, 2017, 7, https://www2.deloitte.com/insights/us/en/focus/human-capital-trends/2017/improving-the-employee-experience-culture-engagement.html.

12. Mat D. Duerden, Peter J. Ward, and Patti A. Freeman, "Conceptualizing Structured Experiences: Seeking Interdisciplinary Integration," *Journal of Leisure Research* 47, no. 5 (2015): 601.

13. *Majstro*, s.v. "*experiri*," http://www.majstro.com/dictionaries/Latin-English/experiri.

14. Duerden, Ward, and Freeman, "Conceptualizing Structured Experiences," 601.

15. Brian Solis, *X: The Experience When Business Meets Design* (Hoboken, NJ: Wiley, 2015), 132.

16. Robert K. Merton, "Resistance to the Systematic Study of Multiple Discoveries in Science," *European Journal of Sociology* 4, no. 2 (1963): 237.

17. B. Joseph Pine II and James Gilmore, "The Roles of the Chief Experience Officer," *AMA Quarterly* (Winter 2017–2018): 5–10.

18. Peter Benz, *Experience Design: Concepts and Case Studies* (London: Bloomsbury, 2014), ix.

19. Harold G. Nelson and Erik Stolterman, *The Design Way: Intentional Change in an Unpredictable World*, 2nd ed. (Cambridge, MA: MIT Press, 2012), 12.

2. What Makes a Great Experience?

1. Adam Alter, *Irresistible: The Rise of Addictive Technology and the Business of Keeping Us Hooked* (New York: Penguin, 2018).

2. Michael J. Ellis, *Why People Play* (Upper Saddle River, NJ: Prentice Hall, 1973).

3. Stuart L. Brown, *Play: How It Shapes the Brain, Opens the Imagination, and Invigorates the Soul* (New York: Avery, 2009).

4. Barry Schwartz, *The Paradox of Choice: Why More Is Less* (New York: HarperCollins, 2004).

5. Mihaly Csikszentmihalyi, *Flow: The Psychology of Optimal Experience* (New York: HarperCollins, 2008).

6. Csikszentmihalyi's work on flow and related concepts directly relates to how experience is operationalized. The material cited here was deduced from his work but is not a direct quotation.

7. The Y (YMCA), "Our Focus," The Y, https://www.ymca.net/our-focus.

8. Martin E. P. Seligman, *Authentic Happiness: Using the New Positive Psychology to Realize Your Potential for Lasting Fulfillment* (New York: Simon & Schuster, 2004).

9. Paul Dolan, *Happiness by Design* (New York: Penguin Random House, 2014), 10.

10. Seligman, *Authentic Happiness*, 42

11. Dolan, *Happiness by Design*, 35.

12. Chip Heath and Dan Heath, *The Power of Moments: Why Certain Experiences Have Extraordinary Impact* (New York: Simon & Schuster, 2017).

13. Martin E. P. Seligman, *Flourish: A Visionary New Understanding of Happiness and Well-Being* (New York: Simon & Schuster, 2012), 16–20.

14. Seligman, *Flourish*, 16.

15. Seligman, *Flourish*, 17.

16. Seligman, *Flourish*, 17.

17. Amy Wrzesniewski, Clark McCauley, Paul Rozin, and Barry Schwartz, "Jobs, Careers, and Callings: People's Relations to Their Work," *Journal of Research in Personality* 31, no. 1 (1997): 21–33.

18. Richard M. Ryan and Edward L. Deci, "Self-Determination Theory and the Facilitation of Intrinsic Motivation, Social Development, and Well-Being," *American Psychologist* 55, no. 1 (2000): 68.

19. Edward L. Deci and Richard M. Ryan, eds., *Handbook of Self-Determination Research*. (Rochester, NY: Univ. Rochester Press, 2002).

20. Daniel Kahneman, *Thinking, Fast and Slow* (London: Macmillan, 2011), 20–21.

21. Heath and Heath, *The Power of Moments*, 11.

22. Richard C. Atkinson and Richard M. Shiffrin, "Human Memory: A Proposed System and Its Control Processes," in *The Psychology of Learning and Motivation*, vol. 2, ed. Kenneth W. Spence and Janet Taylor Spence (New York: Academic Press, 1968), 89.

23. Jennifer Ouellette, "As Time Goes By—Scientists Found Brain's Internal Clock That Influences How We Perceive Time," ARS Technica,

August 31, 2018, 2, https://arstechnica.com/science/2018/08/scientists-found-brains-internal-clock-that-influences-how-we-perceive-time.

24. Rita Elmkvist Nilsen, "How Your Brain Experiences Time," *Gemini Research News*, August 29, 2018, 1, https://geminiresearchnews.com/2018/08/how-your-brain-experiences-time.

25. Albert Tsao, Jørgen Sugar, Li Lu, Cheng Wang, James J. Knierim, May-Britt Moser, and Edvard I. Moser, "Integrating Time from Experience in the Lateral Entorhinal Cortex," *Nature* (San Francisco, CA: Springer Nature, 2018), n.p.

26. Nilsen, "How Your Brain Experiences Time," 2.

27. Nilsen, "How Your Brain Experiences Time," 2.

28. Nilsen, "How Your Brain Experiences Time," 4.

29. B. Joseph Pine II and James H. Gilmore, *The Experience Economy: Work Is Theatre and Every Business a Stage* (Boston: Harvard Business School Press, 1999).

30. B. Joseph Pine II and James H. Gilmore, *The Experience Economy*, updated ed. (Boston: Harvard Business Review Press, 2011).

31. Brian Solis, *X: The Experience When Business Meets Design* (Hoboken, NJ: Wiley, 2015), 10.

32. Pine and Gilmore, *The Experience Economy*, 2.

33. Barry Schwartz, *The Paradox of Choice: Why More Is Less* (New York: HarperCollins, 2004).

34. Pine and Gilmore, *The Experience Economy*, 108–17.

35. Pine and Gilmore, *The Experience Economy*, 101–18.

36. Pine and Gilmore, *The Experience Economy*, 29.

37. Pine and Gilmore, *The Experience Economy*, 30.

38. Josh Bersin, Jason Flynn, Art Mazor, and Veronica Melian, "Rewriting the Rules for the Digital Age," Deloitte Insights, *2017 Global Human Capital Trends*, February 28, 2017, 57, https://www2.deloitte.com/insights/us/en/focus/human-capital-trends/2017/improving-the-employee-experience-culture-engagement.html.

39. *Business Dictionary*, s.v. "production," http://www.businessdictionary.com/definition/production.html.

40. John R. Kelly, *Leisure Business Strategies: What They Don't Teach You in Business School* (Urbana, IL: Sagamore, 2013), 109.

3. A Framework of Experience Types

1. Bernardo Kastrup, Henry P. Stapp, and Menas C. Kafatos, "Coming to Grips with the Implications of Quantum Mechanics," *Scientific American*, May 29, 2018, 3, https://blogs.scientificamerican.com/observations/coming-to-grips-with-the-implications-of-quantum-mechanics.

2. Kastrup, Stapp, and Kafatos, "Implications of Quantum Mechanics," 5.

3. John Dewey, *Art as Experience* (New York: Penguin, 2005).

4. *Merriam-Webster*, s.v. "prosaic," https://www.merriam-webster.com/dictionary/prosaic?utm_campaign=sd&utm_medium=serp&utm_source=jsonld.

5. Daniel Kahneman, *Thinking, Fast and Slow* (London: Macmillan, 2011).

6. Kahneman, *Thinking, Fast and Slow.*

7. Kahneman, *Thinking, Fast and Slow.*

8. Dewey, *Art as Experience.*

9. Kahneman, *Thinking, Fast and Slow.*

10. Personal communication with Bob, who hosted Bill Nye the Science Guy when Bill keynoted Science and Technology Week (Illinois State University, Normal, IL, April 17, 2001).

11. For links to some of the best flight safety videos, check out http://mentalfloss.com/article/67178/11-creative-flight-safety-videos-around-world.

12. Daniel Kahneman and Jason Riis, "Living, and Thinking About It: Two Perspectives on Life," in *The Science of Well-Being*, ed. Felicia A. Huppert, Nick Baylis, and Barry Keverne (Oxford: Oxford Univ. Press, 2005), 285–304.

13. For a good treatment of this topic, check out Daniel Kahneman, *Thinking, Fast and Slow*; and Chip Heath and Dan Heath, *The Power of Moments* (New York: Simon & Schuster, 2017).

14. Heath and Heath, *The Power of Moments*, 11.

15. Martin Miller, "Disney's Lost and Found: Tales of Missing Children Have Happy Endings at Park," *Los Angeles Times*, June 12, 1994, http://articles.latimes.com/1994-06-12/news/mn-3422_1_lost-children.

16. Mary Jo Bitner, Bernard H. Booms, and Mary Stanfield Tetreault, "The Service Encounter: Diagnosing Favorable and Unfavorable Incidents," *Journal of Marketing* 54 (1990): 71–84.

17. Martin E. P. Seligman, *Authentic Happiness: Using the New Positive Psychology to Realize Your Potential for Lasting Fulfillment* (New York: Simon & Schuster, 2004), 8.

18. Charles Dickens, *A Christmas Carol* (London: Bradberry & Evans, 1858), 91.

19. Dickens, *A Christmas Carol*, 91.

20. Dickens, *A Christmas Carol*, 99.

21. Jenkins L. Jones, "Big Rock Candy Mountains," *Deseret News* (Salt Lake City, UT), June 12, 1973, A4.

22. Michael W. Eysenck, *Happiness: Facts and Myths* (Hove, East Sussex, UK: Psychology Press, 1994).

23. P. Brickman, D. Coates, and R. Janoff-Bulman, "Lottery Winners and Accident Victims: Is Happiness Relative?," *Journal of Personality and Social Psychology* 36, no. 8 (1978): 917.

24. Steve Diller, Nathan Shedroff, and Darrel Rhea, *Making Meaning: How Successful Businesses Deliver Meaningful Customer Experiences* (San Francisco: New Riders, 2008), 3.

25. Herbert Blumer, *Symbolic Interactionism: Perspective and Method* (Englewood Cliffs, NJ: Prentice-Hall, 1969).

26. J. Robert Rossman and Barbara E. Schlatter, *Recreation Programming: Designing and Staging Leisure Experiences*, 7th ed. (Urbana, IL: Sagamore, 2015), 28–30.

27. Rossman and Schlatter, *Recreation Programming*, 29.

28. Harlem Globetrotters, *Magic Pass*, accessed September 14, 2018, https://www.harlemglobetrotters.com/magic-pass.

29. Richard Florida, *The Rise of the Creative Class* (New York: Basic Books, 2002), 166–67.

30. Mat D. Duerden, Peter A. Witt, and Stacey Taniguchi, "The Impact of Postprogram Reflection on Recreation Program Results," *Journal of Park and Recreation Administration* 30, no. 1 (2012): 36–50.

31. Arlie R. Hochschild, *The Managed Heart* (Berkeley: Univ. of California Press, 1983), 7.

32. Hochschild, *The Managed Heart*, 21.

33. Tony Schwartz and Catherine McCarthy, "Manage Your Energy, Not Your Time," *Harvard Business Review* 85, no. 10 (2007): 63.

34. David Meerman Scott, *The New Rules of Marketing and PR* (New York: Wiley, 2017), 49.

35. Seligman, *Authentic Happiness*, 102.

36. Seligman, *Authentic Happiness*, 103.

37. Seligman, *Authentic Happiness*, 104.

38. Seligman, *Authentic Happiness*, 111.

39. Seligman, *Authentic Happiness*, 112.

40. Seligman, *Authentic Happiness*, 112.

41. Ting Zhang, "The Personal and Interpersonal Benefits of Rediscovery" (PhD diss., Harvard University, 2015), 22, https://dash.harvard.edu/handle/1/17467290.

42. Zhang, "The Personal and Interpersonal Benefits of Rediscovery." 22.

43. Zhang, "The Personal and Interpersonal Benefits of Rediscovery." 22.

4. The Experiencescape

1. Tom O'Dell and Peter Billing, eds., *Experiencescapes: Tourism, Culture, and Economy* (Herndon, VA: Copenhagen Business School Press, 2005), 16.

2. This term was first used by Bob in a 1996 proposal to the U.S. Navy Morale, Welfare, and Recreation operations for a workshop on

recreation program development and was spelled with the following twist: EXPERIENCESCAPES(QPD), Quality Program Design.

3. O'Dell and Billing, *Experiencescapes*, 16.

4. J. Robert Rossman and Barbara Elwood Schlatter, *Recreation Programming: Designing and Staging Leisure Experiences* (Urbana, IL: Sagamore, 2015), 39–58.

5. Rossman and Schlatter, *Recreation Programming*, 41–52. The genesis of these elements comes from an article by Norman K. Denzin, "Play, Games, and Interaction: The Contexts of Childhood Socialization," *Sociological Quarterly* 16, no. 4 (1975): 458. Denzin drew from the collective works of Erving Goffman, who had spent his career developing a dramaturgical view of sociology that accounted for building society in the everyday occasions of face-to-face interaction. Several of Goffman's works that contributed to this effort are *The Presentation of Self in Everyday Life* (Garden City, NY: Anchor Books, 1956); *Interaction Ritual* (Garden City, NY: Anchor Books, 1967); *Relations in Public* (New York: Harper & Row, 1971); and *Frame Analysis* (New York: Harper & Row, 1974).

6. The following two works examine this phenomenon: Bo Evardsson, Bård Tronvoll, and Thorsten Gruber, "Expanding Understanding of Service Exchange and Value Co-creation: A Social Constructionist Approach," *Journal of the Academy of Marketing Science* 39, no. 2 (2011): 327; Wolff-Michael Roth and Alfredo Jornet, "Towards a Theory of Experience," *Science Education* 90 (2014): 106.

7. Thomas Wendt, *Design for Dasein: Understanding the Design of Experiences* (New York: Wendt, 2015), 16.

8. Wendt, *Design for Dasein*, 16.

9. Albert Tsao, Jørgen Sugar, Li Lu, Cheng Wang, James J. Knierim, May-Britt Moser, and Edvard I. Moser, "Integrating Time from Experience in the Lateral Entorhinal Cortex," *Nature* (San Francisco: Springer Nature, 2018).

10. *Sociology Index*, s.v. "Generalized Other," http://sociologyindex.com/generalized_other.htm.

11. Roth and Jornet, "Towards a Theory of Experience," 106.

12. Claude Romano, *L'evenement et le monde* [Event and world] (Paris: Presses Universitaries de France, 1998), 197. Trans. from French and quoted in Roth and Jornet, "Towards a Theory of Experience," 106.

13. Roth and Jornet, "Towards a Theory of Experience," 106.

14. Nina Simon, *The Participatory Museum* (Santa Cruz, CA: Museum 2.0, 2010).

15. Simon, *The Participatory Museum*, i–ii.

16. David Meerman Scott, *The New Rules of Marketing and PR* (New York: Wiley, 2017), 15.

17. Scott, *New Rules of Marketing*, 9.

18. Scott, *New Rules of Marketing*, n.p.

5. Experience Design Thinking

1. Harold G. Nelson and Erik Stolterman, *The Design Way: Intentional Change in an Unpredictable World*, 2nd ed. (Cambridge, MA: MIT Press, 2012), 12.

2. Daniel Coyle, *The Talent Code: Greatness Isn't Born. It's Grown. Here's How* (New York: Bantam, 2009).

3. Tom Kelley and David Kelley, *Creative Confidence: Unleashing the Creative Potential Within Us All* (New York: Crown Business, 2013).

4. Eric Ries, *The Lean Startup: How Today's Entrepreneurs Use Continuous Innovation to Create Radically Successful Businesses* (New York: Crown Business, 2011).

5. Horst W. J. Rittel and Melvin M. Webber, "Dilemmas in a General Theory of Planning," *Policy Sciences* 4, no. 2 (1973): 155.

6. For more information on design thinking, check out these sources: Hasso Plattner Institute of Design at Stanford, "A Virtual Crash Course in Design Thinking," d.school, https://dschool.stanford.edu/resources-collections/a-virtual-crash-course-in-design-thinking; "Design Thinking," IDEO, https://www.ideou.com/pages/design-thinking.

7. Hasso Plattner Institute of Design at Stanford, "An Introduction to Design Thinking Process Guide," d.school, 3, https://dschool-old.stanford.edu/sandbox/groups/designresources/wiki/36873/attachments/74b3d/StageGuideBOOTCAMP2010L.pdf.

8. *Merriam-Webster*, s.v. "empathy," https://www.merriam-webster.com/dictionary/empathy.

9. Mat D. Duerden, Peter J. Ward, and Patti A. Freeman, "Conceptualizing Structured Experiences: Seeking Interdisciplinary Integration," *Journal of Leisure Research* 47, no. 5 (2015): 601.

10. The list of participant elements compiled by Duerden, Ward, and Freeman was built on the work of the following researchers: Elizabeth C. Hirschman and Morris B. Holbrook, "Expanding the Ontology and Methodology of Research on the Consumption Experience," in *Perspectives on Methodology in Consumer Research*, ed. David Brinberg and Richard J. Lutz (New York: Springer Verlag, 1986), 213; and J. Robert Rossman and Barbara E. Schlatter, *Recreation Programming: Designing and Staging Leisure Experiences*, 7th ed. (Urbana, IL: Sagamore, 2015).

11. Clayton M. Christensen, Scott D. Anthony, Gerald Berstell, and Denise Nitterhouse, "Finding the Right Job for Your Product," *MIT Sloan Management Review* 48, no. 3 (2007): 38.

12. John Connors, in discussion with Mat Duerden, October 2013.

13. Hasso Plattner Institute, "An Introduction to Design Thinking," 3.

14. Dave Gray, "Update to the Empathy Map," July 18, 2017, Gamestorming, http://gamestorming.com/update-to-the-empathy-map.

15. Hasso Plattner Institute of Design at Stanford, "The Bootcamp Bootleg," 21, d.school, https://static1.squarespace.com/static/57c6b79629687fde090a0fdd/t/58890239db29d6cc6c3338f7/1485374014340/METHODCARDS-v3-slim.pdf.

16. Hasso Plattner Institute, "The Bootcamp Bootleg."

17. Hasso Plattner Institute, "The Bootcamp Bootleg."

18. Thomas Wendt, *Design for Dasein: Understanding the Design of Experiences* (New York: Wendt, 2015), 9.

19. Wendt, *Design for Dasein*, 73.

20. Karen Collias, "Unpacking Design Thinking: Ideate," August 3, 2014, Knowledge Without Borders, http://knowwithoutborders.org/unpacking-design-thinking-ideate.

21. Hasso Plattner Institute, "The Bootcamp Bootleg," 30.

22. Hasso Plattner Institute, "The Bootcamp Bootleg," 30.

23. Eric Ries, *The Lean Startup: How Today's Entrepreneurs Use Continuous Innovation to Create Radically Successful Businesses* (New York: Crown Business, 2011), 4.

24. Hasso Plattner Institute, "An Introduction to Design Thinking," 7.

25. Seymour Papert and Idit Harel, *Constructionism* (Norwood, NJ: Ablex, 1991).

26. Rossman and Schlatter, *Recreation Programming*.

6. Designing the Experience Journey

1. Jason Cohen, "Holy Crap," *Texas Monthly*, October 2013, www.texasmonthly.com/travel/holy-crap.

2. Theodore Kinni, *Be Our Guest: Perfecting the Art of Customer Service*, rev. ed. (New York: Disney Press, 2011), 23.

3. Kinni, *Be Our Guest*, 23.

4. The following two sources discuss various types of experience maps: James Kalbach, *Mapping Experiences: A Complete Guide to Creating Value Through Journeys, Blueprints, and Diagrams* (Sebastopol, CA: O'Reilly Media, 2016); Brian Solis, *X: The Experience When Business Meets Design* (Hoboken, NJ: Wiley, 2015).

5. Kalbach, *Mapping Experiences*, 89.

6. Kalbach, *Mapping Experiences*, 91.

7. Chip Heath and Dan Heath, *The Power of Moments* (New York: Simon & Schuster, 2017).

8. Solis, *When Business Meets Design*.

9. John Connors, Mat Duerden, Peter Ward, and Brian Hill, "Creating Lasting Customer Relationships: Lessons Learned from The Color Run" (workshop at the National Recreation and Parks Association Conference, Las Vegas, NV, 2015).

10. Connors, Duerden, Ward, and Hill, "Creating Lasting Customer Relationships."

11. Heather Long, "Disney World Secrets," Love to Know, http://themeparks.lovetoknow.com/Disney_World_Secrets.

12. Designing CX, "CX Journey Mapping Workshop Slides," Designing CX, http://designingcx.com/cx-journey-mapping-toolkit.

13. Designing CX, "CX Journey Mapping Workshop Slides."

14. B. Joseph Pine II and James H. Gilmore, *The Experience Economy*, updated ed. (Boston: Harvard Business Review Press, 2011).

7. Touchpoints and Transitions

1. J. Robert Rossman and Barbara E. Schlatter, *Recreation Programming: Designing and Staging Leisure Experiences*, 7th ed. (Urbana, IL: Sagamore, 2015), 217–26.

2. Stephen R. Covey, *The 8th Habit* (New York: Free Press, 2004), 152.

3. *Business Dictionary*, s.v. "co-creation," www.businessdictionary.com/definition/co-creation.html.

4. Coimbatore K. Prahalad and Venkat Ramaswamy, "Co-creation Experiences: The Next Practice in Value Creation," *Journal of Interactive Marketing* 18, no. 3 (2004): 6.

5. Prahalad and Ramaswamy, "Co-creation Experiences," 9.

6. Clay Shirky, *Cognitive Surplus: Creativity and Generosity in a Connected Age* (New York: Penguin, 2010), 58.

7. Younger readers may not know of *Cheers* or its impact. It was one of the most successful sitcoms ever on TV, running from September 30, 1982, to May 20, 1993, with a total of 275 half-hour episodes for eleven seasons. Norm, Cliff, and Frasier were bar customers who added value to coming to Cheers, the bar where "everybody knows your name." The series was so popular that you can still go to a Cheers bar in Boston that celebrates the series. You can learn more at https://en.wikipedia.org/wiki/Cheers.

8. If you are ever in Buenos Aires, you too can participate by contacting Mrs. Soued at the following e-mail address: normasoued@gmail.com. You can see pictures of the class at http://argentinecookingclasses.com.

9. CBS News, "Falconry and Fire-Swallowing: How Airbnb's 'Experiences' Are Transforming the Platform," CBS News, August 29, 2018, https://www.cbsnews.com/news/airbnb-experiences-provide-boost-for-platform.

10. Andrew Lacanienta and Mat Duerden, "Designing and Staging High Quality Park and Recreation Experiences Using Co-Creation," *Journal of Park and Recreation Administration* (in press).

11. Pine and Gilmore call this concept "customer sacrifice." B. Joseph Pine II and James H. Gilmore, *The Experience Economy*, updated ed. (Boston: Harvard Business Review Press, 2011).

8. The Stories We Tell: Building Drama in Your Experiences

1. Charles Dickens, *A Tale of Two Cities* (London: Nisbet, 1902), 3.

2. J. R. R. Tolkien, *The Hobbit* (New York: Houghton Mifflin Harcourt, 2001), 1.

3. *Star Wars, Episode IV: A New Hope*, directed by George Lucas (Los Angeles: 20th Century Fox, 1977).

4. Coimbatore K. Prahalad and Venkat Ramaswamy, "Co-creation Experiences: The Next Practice in Value Creation," *Journal of Interactive Marketing* 18, no. 3 (2004): 5.

5. Emily Esfahani Smith, *The Power of Meaning: Creating a Life That Matters* (New York: Crown, 2017), 41.

6. Smith, *The Power of Meaning*, 104.

7. Brian Solis, *X: The Experience When Business Meets Design* (Hoboken, NJ: Wiley, 2015).

8. Devin Leonard and Christopher Palmeri, "Disney's Intergalactic Theme Park Quest to Beat Harry Potter," *Bloomberg Businessweek*, April 19, 2017, https://www.bloomberg.com/news/features/2017-04-19/disney-s-intergalactic-theme-park-quest-to-beat-harry-potter.

9. Leonard and Palmeri, "Disney's Intergalactic Theme Park Quest."

10. Leonard and Palmeri, "Disney's Intergalactic Theme Park Quest."

11. Gustav Freytag, *Freytag's Technique of the Drama: An Exposition of Dramatic Composition and Art*, trans. Elias J. MacEwan (Chicago: S. C. Griggs, 1895).

12. Joseph Campbell, *The Hero with a Thousand Faces*, 3rd ed. (Novato, CA: New World Library, 2008).

13. Christopher Vogler, "A Practical Guide to Joseph Campbell's *The Hero with a Thousand Faces*," *The Writer's Journey*, 1985, http://www.thewritersjourney.com/hero%27s_journey.htm#Memo.

14. Alex Ferrari, "The Power of Myth: Creating Star Wars' Mythos with Joseph Campbell," Indie Film Hustle, December 7, 2017, 3, https://indiefilmhustle.com/the-power-of-myth-star-wars-joseph-campbell.

15. Google Search Stories, "Parisian Love," YouTube video, https://www.youtube.com/watch?v=nnsSUqgkDwU.

16. For an excellent discussion of theming, see chapter 3 in B. Joseph Pine II and James H. Gilmore, *The Experience Economy*, updated ed. (Boston: Harvard Business Review Press, 2011).

17. For some great insights on the power of constraints to fuel creativity, read Tom Kelly and David Kelly, *Creative Confidence: Unleashing the Creative Potential Within Us All* (New York: Crown Business, 2013), 126–29.

18. Polynesian Cultural Center, "About Us," Polynesian Cultural Center, www.polynesia.com/FAQ-About-Us.html#.WU2vEsbMx0s.

19. Polynesian Cultural Center, "About," Hukilau Marketplace, http://hukilaumarketplace.com/about.

20. Mike Lee, personal communication with Mat. Mike Lee serves on the advisory board for the Department of Experience Design and Management in the Marriott School of Business at Brigham Young University, Provo, UT, where Mat teaches.

21. Anastasia Kreposhina (project manager, IKEA Centres Russia), personal communication with Mat, November 9, 2016.

22. Scott Lukas, *The Immersive Worlds Handbook: Designing Theme Parks and Consumer Spaces* (New York: Focal Press, 2013).

9. Techniques for Enhancing Experiences

1. Christopher Carroll, Malcolm Patterson, Stephen Wood, Andrew Booth, Jo Rick, and Shashi Balain, "A Conceptual Framework for Implementation Fidelity," *Implementation Science* 2, no. 1 (2007): 40.

2. B. Joseph Pine II and James H. Gilmore, *The Experience Economy*, updated ed. (Boston, MA: Harvard Business Review Press, 2011).

3. For more information on the work of these individuals, see Anantharanthan Parasuraman, Valarie A. Zeithaml, and Leonard L. Berry, "SERVQUAL: A Multiple-Item Scale for Measuring Consumer Perceptions," *Journal of Retailing* 64, no. 1 (1988): 12; and Anantharanthan Parasuraman, Leonard L. Berry, and Valarie A. Zeithaml, "Refinement and Reassessment of the SERVQUAL Scale," *Journal of Retailing* 67, no. 4 (1991): 420.

4. Gary D. Ellis and J. Robert Rossman, "Creating Value for Participants Through Experience Staging: Parks, Recreation, and Tourism in the Experience Industry," *Journal of Park and Recreation Administration* 26, no. 4 (2008): 1.

5. Ellis and Rossman, "Creating Value for Participants," 10.

6. *Merriam-Webster*, s.v. "service," https://www.merriam-webster.com/dictionary/service.

7. Parasuraman, Zeithaml, and Berry, "SERVQUAL," 12.

8. Daniel Victor and Matt Stevens, "United Airlines Passenger Is Dragged from an Overbooked Flight," *New York Times*, April 19, 2017, https://www.nytimes.com/2017/04/10/business/united-flight-passenger-dragged.html?_r=0.

9. Mary Jo Bitner, Bernard H. Booms, and Mary Stanfield Tetreault, "The Service Encounter: Diagnosing Favorable and Unfavorable Incidents," *Journal of Marketing* 54 (1990): 71–84.

10. Seth King, Sam Williams, and Callan Graham, "Lessons Learned Designing Questival," Keynote Address, Experience Design Quest, Brigham Young University, Provo, Utah, April 14, 2018.

11. Pine and Gilmore, *The Experience Economy*, updated ed.

12. Pine and Gilmore, *The Experience Economy*, updated ed.

13. David Meerman Scott, *The New Rules of Marketing and PR* (New York: Wiley, 2017), 49.

14. B. Joseph Pine II, *Mass Customization: The New Frontier in Business Competition* (Boston: Harvard Business School Press, 1993).

15. Barry Schwartz, *The Paradox of Choice: Why Less Is More* (New York: Ecco, 2004).

16. David Kelley and Tom Kelley, *Creative Confidence: Unleashing the Creative Potential Within Us All* (New York: Crown Business, 2013).

17. Parasuraman, Berry, and Zeithaml, "Refinement and Reassessment of the SERVQUAL Scale."

18. Chip Heath and Dan Heath, *The Power of Moments: Why Certain Experiences Have Extraordinary Impact* (New York: Simon & Schuster, 2017).

19. Heath and Heath, *The Power of Moments.*

20. Pine and Gilmore, *The Experience Economy*, updated ed.

21. We are grateful to an anonymous reviewer who evidently attends a lot more weddings than we do and brought us up to date about wedding practices these days.

22. Joe Coscarelli and Melena Ryzik, "Fyre Festival, a Luxury Music Weekend, Crumbles in the Bahamas," *New York Times*, April 28, 2017, https://www.nytimes.com/2017/04/28/arts/music/fyre-festival-ja-rule-bahamas.html.

23. See the following articles for more information on the Fyre Festival fallout: Jonathan Randles, "Fyre Festival Placed in Bankruptcy After Lending Pressure," *Wall Street Journal*, August 30, 2017, https://www.wsj.com/articles/fyre-festival-placed-in-bankruptcy-after-lender-pressure-1504130632; Amy B. Wang, "Founder of Disastrous Fyre Festival Arrested, Charged with Fraud," *Washington Post*, July 1, 2017, https://www.washingtonpost.com/news/arts-and-entertainment/wp/2017/07/01/founder-of-disastrous-fyre-festival-arrested-and-charged-with-fraud/; Lizzie Plaugic, "Ja Rule's Catastrophic Fyre Festival Gets a Documentary Series on Hulu," *The Verge*, April 16, 2018, https://www.theverge.com/2018/4/16/17243802/hulu-fyre-festival-documentary-series-ja-rule-billy-mcfarland.

10. Using Experience Design in Product Development and Corporate Strategy

1. B. Joseph Pine II and James Gilmore, "The Roles of the Chief Experience Officer," *AMA Quarterly* (Winter 2017–2018): 5–10.

2. Fox Restaurant Concepts, "About Us," Fox Restaurant Concepts, https://www.foxrc.com/about-us.

3. Fox Restaurant Concepts, "About Us."

4. B. Joseph Pine II and James H. Gilmore, *The Experience Economy*, updated ed. (Boston: Harvard Business Review Press, 2011).

5. Brinker International, "Making People Feel Special," *Brinker International*, http://www.brinker.com/company/default.html.

6. Wayne, T. Roberts, "2016 Annual Report," *Brinker International*, 2, https://www.proxydocs.com/edocs/request?b=EAT&paction=doc&action=showdoc&docid=1053778&se=1053778.

7. Roberts, "2016 Annual Report."

8. Elizabeth Weise, "Amazon's Checkout-Free Amazon Go Stores Coming to San Francisco and Chicago," *USA Today*, May 14, 2018, https://www.usatoday.com/story/tech/talkingtech/2018/05/14/checkout-free-amazon-go-stores-coming-san-francisco-chicago/609794002.

9. Hasbro, "Corporate," Hasbro, https://hasbro.gcs-web.com/corporate.

10. Anne Quito, "Why Hasbro Trademarked Play-Doh's Scent," *Quartz*, May 28, 2018, https://qz.com/1290460/why-hasbro-trademarked-play-dohs-scent.

11. Jennifer Fickley-Baker, "*Star Wars*–Inspired Resort Planned for Walt Disney World Resort Promises to Be 'Unlike Anything That Exists Today,' " *Disney Parks Blog*, February 11, 2018, https://disneyparks.disney.go.com/blog/2018/02/d23j-update-star-wars-hotel.

12. Holland America Line, "About Us," Holland America Line, https://www.hollandamerica.com/en_US/our-company/mission-values.html.

13. Lennar, "Simplicity," Lennar, https://www.lennar.com/ei/simplicity.

14. Kris Frieswick, "Deals on Wheels," *National Geographic*, May 19, 2018, https://www.nationalgeographic.com/travel/features/far-and-away/deals-on-wheels.

Conclusion

1. Just Disney, "Walt's Private Apartment," *Just Disney*, http://www.justdisney.com/features/apartment.html.

Index